For Better or For ~~Worse~~ Best!

Building Your Marriage Heart-to-Heart

Tom & Alane Waters

Coldwater, Michigan 49036
www.remnantpublications.com

Copyright © 2011 by Tom and Alane Waters
All Rights Reserved

Printed in the USA

Published by
Remnant Publications
649 East Chicago Road
Coldwater MI 49036
517-279-1304
www.remnantpublications.com

All Bible quotations are taken from the
King James Version, unless otherwise noted.

Bible quotations marked NKJV are taken from
the *New King James Version*. Copyright © 1982 by
Thomas Nelson, Inc. Used by permission. All rights reserved.

Cover Design by David Berthiaume
Text Edit by Tarah Solie Benton
Text Design by Greg Solie • AltamontGraphics.com

ISBN 978-1-933291-70-3

Contents

Foreword 5
1. Great Expectations. 7
2. Minor—and Major—Adjustments 11
3. A Jolt to My Own Perspective 17
4. Two "Me's" or One "Us"? (Part I) 19
5. Two "Me's" or One "Us"? (Part II) 23
6. Building a Sure Foundation. 31
7. An Enduring Commitment. 35
8. Effective Communication. 41
9. Communication Breakers. 53
10. Respect and Restraint 61
11. Setting Goals and Priorities. 73
12. Moral Purity for Men 81
13. Moral Purity for Women 85
14. Mutually Meaningful Intimacy. 89
15. Finding Forgiveness. 93
16. Money Matters. 99
17. Managing Emotions. .109
18. Resolving Conflict. 115
19. Keeping Love Alive 121

Foreword

I could hardly believe it. Tom and I had just spent the night and most of the early morning hours in vulnerable, heart-searching prayer. Neither one of us had ever done anything like that before. An hour was just about my limit. Yet, the time flew by as if we were talking to Jesus face to face.

What started out as just a short prayer for each of us ended six fantastic hours later! I knew without a doubt that there was absolutely nothing between my Savior and me.

"What in the world could you pray about for so long?" you might ask. It was about us, our wives, our children, and our friends. The majority of our prayers were about letting go of all those little pet sins that so often beset us in our walk with God. Sins that were, and still are, so much a part of us, that when we saw them for what they were and how they affected our relationships with others, we didn't want them anymore. It was amazing what happened when we were totally honest with God and ourselves. We asked Him to reveal anything—and I mean anything—that was keeping us from having the walk and communion with God that we so desperately needed. When the prayers finally ended, Tom and I agreed that we had never before felt so squeaky clean on the inside and the outside! That night's experience with God caused us to become better men, husbands, and fathers.

After rooming together in a church boarding academy, Tom and I have known each other for many years. When we went our separate ways from school, we both had plans. Unfortunately, those plans did not include God being in charge in either of our lives. Back then, if you had asked either one of us about marriage, we would have said that the only thing between us and a perfect marriage was finishing school,

For Better or For ~~Worse~~ Best

making some money, and finding the "right" gal. We might have told you that we had a lot to offer in marriage.

If you would have asked us about spiritual leadership in a relationship, we probably would have laughed. Had you asked about conflict-resolution skills, we probably would have wondered why we would need *those*. After all, what girl would ever have any sort of a conflict with either of us? Questions about communication and listening skills would have also been met with a "no problem." Why wouldn't we want to listen to the beautiful wife we imagined? Had you asked us about the circle of love and respect that is such an integral part of the marriage relationship, we probably would have thought you were trying to put a square peg into a round hole. This was about as deep as it went for us with the divine relationship of marriage. I think that's also about as deep as it gets with marriage for many other couples.

The great news is that it doesn't have to be that way! This book, *For Better or for Best,* will give you the nuts and bolts of how a *"Best"* marriage can happen. This book is so practical, which is one of the reasons why I love it. It also makes good, old-fashioned sense. When you put the principles of God's Word together with the common sense in this book and implement them in your marriage, I guarantee that it will work! How can I be so sure? It is because I have seen the principles in this book put into living action. Having been in Tom and Alane's home many times as their children were growing up, and having attended their seminars, I saw these principles working in their lives. My wife Deb and I also applied and used these same principles, and they just plain work.

If you desire all that your wedding day promised, and you are willing to seek God as the center of your marriage then **this book is for you and your spouse!**

Dwight Hall

Dwight Hall
Founder, Remnant Publications
Reaching the World One Book at a Time

Chapter One

Great Expectations

"Marriage sure isn't what I bargained for," I grumbled while storming around the house. On what could have been a quiet, contented evening, Alane and I had just engaged in another of our all-out spats. Though still newlyweds, fights and squabbles had become the norm for us, and I was sick of it all.

"Alane is so selfish!" my angry thoughts raged on. "She's a good cook, but she is so negative now, where's the vivacious girl I thought I married?"

Wanting to be by myself, I grabbed some paperwork and headed towards our home office. The last person I wanted to see at that moment was Alane, and I thought she was in the kitchen. As I stepped into the office, however, I realized I wasn't alone. There she was, huddled in a corner, weeping. I was too angry to feel any sympathy. Whirling around, I stomped out. Frustrated that even the sanctuary of my office had been invaded by tears, I retreated into the basement and lapsed into a now-familiar routine of self-pity and rehearsing *her* problems.

"Here we go again!" I groused. "How irritating it is that I'm forced to endure her negative mood swings." As furious as I was, the sorrowful sight I had just witnessed in the office also began playing through my mind. There was Alane, the beautiful girl I had so recently promised to cherish, huddled back in a corner. The thought of her trembling and sobbing, the idea of her feeling so unappreciated and unloved, shocked even my angry heart.

"How did it come to this?" I wondered. "We're still newlyweds. We should be deeply in love—not fighting our way through marriage!"

Our relationship certainly hadn't started out in this vein. We first met at work, where I was the evening supervisor of a hospital radiology

For Better or For ~~Worse~~ Best

department and Alane was the new nurse recruiter. The first time we saw each other was when she delivered the new employee handbook. It wasn't love at first sight for either of us, but I was definitely attracted to her.

Having asked God to guide me in my next relationship, I prayed about whether or not I should ask her out. When I felt I had God's permission, I was really surprised when she turned me down. Though she had a prior commitment, my pride still felt the sting. I did respect her for not being willing to break her other appointment, however.

I didn't ask Alane out again for another six months, but during that time, we served as co-leaders of the young-adult division of our church. The opportunity to work together in a non-dating relationship proved to be a great blessing, as Alane and I were able to observe each other's thought processes, organizational skills, and ability to work under difficult circumstances in regular, daily activities. There were no expectations to meet—just a normal situation—and opportunity to get truly acquainted.

As Alane and I spent more time together, I began to appreciate her many gifts. I also felt increasingly attracted to her. When we finally did have a formal "date," we discovered that we had both felt drawn to each other. Things progressed rather quickly from there. It wasn't long before I asked her to be my wife.

During our engagement, my love for Alane continued to grow. I loved to be with her, and we spent every moment we could together. When we were apart, we frequently talked on the phone. At that point in our relationship, we could talk about anything and everything—or so it seemed.

Our wedding day was a joyful one—though I also admit to some heart-pounding nervousness. As I stood in front of the church, looking back at the double doors, knowing that in a moment my beautiful bride would walk through and become my wife, my heart pounded so hard I wondered if our guests could see it pulsing through my tuxedo!

The wedding went smoothly—the perfect start to what we anticipated would be a new and beautiful life together. We had taken our time in our courtship. We had gotten to know each other, asked for God's guidance, and felt His leading. More than that, we had fallen

Great Expectations

deeply in love. With Alane, I shared the expectation that we would experience an ongoing relationship of harmony and love—"happily ever after." Though I had seen some of the hard times and fighting some of my friends had experienced in their marriages, I felt sure that ours would be different ... we would be the happiest couple ever!

Yet now there was Alane, holed up in our office, crying as if her heart was about to break. And here I was, filled with anger, self-pity, and grief.

"Oh, what has become of our beautiful marriage?" I sank into a couch in the basement and buried my head in my hands.

Chapter Two

Minor—and Major—Adjustments

I was 22 years old when I moved from southern California to a suburb of Chicago to work as the nurse recruiter for a large hospital. Though energetic and excited about my new job opportunity, I only knew one person at the hospital when I first started my job. I soon met Tom, who came to my office a few days later and asked me out for a date. I was surprised he even remembered my name!

I was interested in getting to know Tom better, but had promised some new friends to come watch slides of their family vacation on Saturday night. My parents had taught me the importance of honoring commitments, so I determined to be a person of my word.

"I already have other plans," I told Tom, assuring him that I would be happy to take a rain check. He didn't ask me out again for another six months ...

During that time we became co-leaders in the youth department of our church. I learned a lot about Tom, his character and personality, and most of all his commitment to God during that time. I began to feel drawn to him. Though I previously had the opportunity to date other young men, I had never had this feeling before. But though my attraction to him continued to grow, he had not asked me out again or shown any further interest in me. Because of this, I began praying that God would take away my feelings for Tom, if he was not the right person for me.

Then one evening my telephone rang, and it was Tom. After a brief conversation, he asked me out for the following night. It didn't take us long to discover, on that date, that we had both felt drawn to each other. Instinctively we knew that God had brought us together to become husband and wife. Soon after we came to this realization, Tom proposed. I was thrilled and confident that he was the one for me.

For Better or For ~~Worse~~ Best

"I'd be honored to be your wife," I told him.

Knowing that I would be with Tom for the rest of my life, I looked forward to our wedding day with great joy and anticipation. I loved him and enjoyed spending every spare moment with him. We were learning to become one in heart, mind, and soul. Tom was fun, intelligent, handsome, athletic, serious, and had direction in life. I felt so blessed, knowing that God had brought us together.

Our wedding—on April 13, 1980—went smoothly. Our family and friends had all come to share in our joy. We had our pictures taken before the wedding so our guests wouldn't have to wait after the ceremony. That choice also gave us time to enjoy some special moments before our wedding. I remember standing in the balcony looking down into the sanctuary with Tom's hand on mine thinking, "In just a few minutes we will be married, together for life." This brought unspeakable joy to my heart.

Then the long-awaited moment arrived. I wasn't nervous at all—never had a caution or second thought. I knew Tom was the man for me. Eagerly and joyfully I stood outside the sanctuary, waiting for the note to be struck and those large doors to swing open so I could walk up the aisle and pledge myself, my love, and my life to him.

In just a few minutes we were standing hand in hand at the altar, looking into each other's eyes and vowing to "love, comfort, honor, cherish, to have and to hold from this day forward." The vows continued, "for better or for worse, for richer for poorer, in sickness and in health, in prosperity or adversity, forsaking all others, as long as we both shall live ... till death do us part." With all sincerity, honesty, and love I gladly and eagerly said, "I do!"

Tom had planned a special surprise for me. For our first night together, he had reserved the honeymoon suite at a nearby luxury hotel. When we arrived, however, we found there was no record of his reservation! In fact, our suite was already occupied by another couple. Needless to say, Tom was less than pleased. For the first time ever I saw irritation in him. He finally agreed to take another room—what else could he do?

That night Tom read 1 Corinthians 13, the Bible's "love chapter," to me from a book he had found that contained 31 different versions. And so we began on our wedding night a beautiful habit which would follow

Minor—and Major—Adjustments

every night thereafter: "Love is patient, love is kind." *Touched to see his care, interest, and leadership, I looked forward even more joyfully to a wonderful and happy life together!*

Though delightful in many regards, our honeymoon was not without additional challenges. Tom had planned a trip to Hilton Head Island in South Carolina. He had arranged for a limousine to pick us up, but when it arrived, it turned out to be an old rusted-out 15-passenger van with the word "Limousine" on the side. Tom couldn't believe that this was our "limo," but when the driver got out and held up a white cardboard sign with "Waters" written in black felt-tip letters, reality set in.

"I ordered a limousine," Tom grumbled to the man. "A shiny, posh limo—not a van."

"What does it say?" the man replied curtly, pointing to the proclamation on the side of the van. "Get in and I'll take you to Hilton Head!" Once again—for the second time in our first two days of marriage—I saw Tom flair with irritation.

We tried to rent a car when we reached Hilton Head Island, but were told that we were too young. We were old enough for marriage but too young to rent a car! We ended up renting bicycles and rode all over the island.

Tom had looked forward to playing tennis with me on our honeymoon. Winter weather and working opposite shifts had kept us from playing during our courtship, but I had told him that I enjoyed tennis and that I was a fairly good player.

I'll never forget our first time on the court together. Running frantically from side to side, I was trying to hit the ball but missing most of the time. On the rare occasion I did make contact, the ball usually went out of bounds. The harder I tried, the worse I played. My self-confidence quickly waned, and soon I was feeling intimidated.

It was then that Tom made the fatal statement: "I thought you said you could play tennis!"

That really wounded my pride. It was evident I was just making a fool of myself.

"I thought I could!" I responded as a flood of feelings and emotions rushed to the surface. "At least that's what my old boyfriend always told me. He said I was a good player. I'm just too tired." Tom and I tried

For Better or For ~~Worse~~ Best

playing tennis one more time, but it also ended with my feelings hurt and Tom in a state of frustration.

With tennis no longer an option, Tom and I decided to go canoeing.

"I'm not a good swimmer," I warned him. In fact, I was pretty fearful of water and had only canoed once in my life.

"We will be safe," he reassured me. "We're going to have a great time." Our canoe rental included two life jackets and, upon receiving mine, I immediately put it on and cinched it up.

"What are you doing?" Tom was incredulous. The answer seemed obvious enough to me.

"I'm putting on my life jacket!" I responded, with more than a little sarcasm in my voice.

My only other experience in a canoe had been years before at summer camp with a group of girls, all of whom could swim except me. They thought it would be fun to tip the canoe over. I was totally caught off guard! When I fell into the river the canoe hit me on the back of the head, nearly knocking me out. I fought desperately to keep my head above water. To this day, I'm not sure how I got back to the canoe.

Tom and I started down the river with him in the back and me in the front of the canoe. I had intended to help paddle but found myself clinging to the sides of the canoe. Anytime it got a bit tipsy, feelings of panic swept over me. Tom couldn't understand what was wrong until I blurted out my fearful experience.

"Everything will be fine," he tried to reassure me. I was so consumed with terror, however, that our outing was ruined. Needless to say, we only went canoeing once.

As a last resort we decided to go for a bicycle ride. I did fine with that, though I did have trouble keeping up with him on the hills. He is naturally athletic and I have to work at it.

During our honeymoon activities, we began to see flaws and weaknesses in each other. We had a good time overall, but were already falling into a cycle of blaming each other for our trials while trying to defend ourselves.

When Tom and I returned to real life with the pressures of work, demands of selfishness, and expectations of others—things started to change. We were beginning to learn things about each other that we

Minor—and Major—Adjustments

hadn't seen before. Tom began to verbalize some things that were bothering him, and I reacted with emotion. Soon our communication grew strained. Just a few weeks after our honeymoon, I noticed that he wasn't talking much on our way into work. At church get-togethers and with our friends, Tom always seemed to have plenty to say. But on our way home, he would drop into silence again.

"Why don't you talk to me on the way to work anymore?" I finally asked, after an unsuccessful attempt to generate conversation. It was a question from deep within my heart—a hurting heart that was consumed with thoughts like:

- *"I wonder what's wrong with me."*
- *"Maybe I'm just not important to him."*
- *"I wonder if he really loves me."*

"I'm just not a morning person," Tom replied matter-of-factly.
"Then why don't you talk to me on the way home?" I wanted to know.

My insecurities were beginning to grow, and with them, wrong feelings. Those feelings led me to often respond to him with sharpness and sarcasm or silence and tears, further compounding our problems. It didn't seem like I could do anything right. It came to the point that sometimes when Tom walked into the kitchen, I would feel so stressed that my hands would begin to tremble. That's pretty much where things stood when he and I had "the big fight."

Once again our feelings—and words—had escalated. When Tom stormed downstairs, I huddled in the corner of the office, sobbing quietly. I felt so unloved and unappreciated, I just really wanted to hide. As thoughts over the recent upset tumbled through my mind, I became more and more emotional and grieved.

I thought of how I had left the house after a previous misunderstanding, thinking that "this will teach him! He'll miss me, be worried, and feel bad for the way he treated me." I thought that when I got home, Tom would apologize. Then we'd make up and be happy. I went shopping—something I loved to do—but this time, I hated every minute of it. Realizing how mean I was, I started to feel very guilty and decided to go back home.

For Better or For ~~Worse~~ Best

"Honey, I'm sorry I spoke to you that way. I love you!" were the words I was hoping to hear.

"I'm sorry I left without saying anything," was how I planned to respond. "That was terrible. Please forgive me!" I had it all planned in my mind.

Unfortunately, when I returned home and found out that Tom hadn't even missed me, I was even more hurt and upset than before. Instead of asking for forgiveness for my childish, selfish ways, I got angry with him and accused him of not even caring. Now here I was in a corner, crying my eyes out. Tom had seen it, and stormed downstairs again.

"What is happening to us?" I wondered. "This isn't happily ever after. Why can't we get along, and why doesn't he love me?" Feeling hurt and very ashamed of my childish response, I felt like I couldn't even get up.

Chapter Three

A Jolt to My Own Perspective

It should have broken my heart when I saw Alane crying in that corner, but it didn't. Instead, I felt more frustrated than ever. "That proves it!" I thought. "There is something wrong with her!"

It wasn't until I sank into the basement couch and started thinking that God's Spirit broke through the blindness of my selfish heart. The thoughts that came to me right then rang so loudly in my mind that it could just as well have been the audible voice of God.

"If you don't stop picking on your wife you're going to destroy her!"

What a jolt that was to my own self-centered perspective! What an awakening of reality and truth! Instantly I knew it was God and I knew He was right. I recognized it and accepted it.

Then another clear, practical thought came to me. "Write down ten things that you love and appreciate about your wife." At that point, my tender Heavenly Father really had my attention! I saw my need and I wanted to cooperate with Him. I also realized just how far my faulty, critical thinking had taken me. I couldn't think of anything positive about Alane, except that she was a good cook. And I knew that complimenting her skills in the kitchen had become overused and unappreciated. I cried out to the Lord to open my mind and help me remember what I loved and appreciated about her. God delights to answer such a prayer. He loves to answer the cry of our hearts to do His will!

Almost immediately my mind began to open. It was as though the scales were falling from my eyes. Very quickly, the reasons why I loved and appreciated Alane began to flow onto my paper. The more I wrote, the more excited I became, not only about what was happening in my own heart but about this new sensitivity I was feeling toward my wife who was sitting alone in our office. I wanted to run upstairs and tell

For Better or For ~~Worse~~ Best

her all the wonderful things I loved and appreciated about her. But the same "still, small voice" that prompted me to list her attributes said, "No, you are to demonstrate how you feel about her."

It became clear to me that the first thing I needed to do was confess and repent of the way I'd been treating my dear wife. Then, rather than read a wonderful list of words to her, I needed to allow God to give me the power to live out a demonstration of those words to her—those things I loved and appreciated about her as my wife.

I knew I had hurt Alane deeply—that at that very moment, as far as I knew, she was still huddled upstairs in the corner of the office, crying. For weeks now, our attempts at communication had become more and more tense and sarcastic. I wanted to change all of that, and felt God had shown me the way.

Now only one question remained—how would she respond?

Chapter Four

Two "Me's" or One "Us"? (Part I)

I was still in the corner of our office when I heard the sound of footsteps coming up the stairs. Somehow I felt like Tom might be looking for me—yet wondered if he even cared.

"My reaction just now—of hurt, shame, and embarrassment—only confirms his negative view of me," I thought. Yet as Tom stood in the doorway, I sensed something different about him. Walking slowly across the room, he knelt by my side and took me into his arms.

"Honey, I'm sorry for how I've been treating you," he whispered into my ear. "I do love you and want to be a better husband."

I looked up into his face and saw compassion and love. This broke my stubborn heart.

"I'm sorry, too," I told him. "I really do love you, and want to be a good wife."

Tom then told me of his experience in the basement, adding that from now on, he was going to demonstrate all the reasons he loved me.

"And being a good cook is not one of them," he assured me, as he knew that one had been worn out some time before. That broke the final barrier, and we laughed together as he helped me up. From that day forward we started the real journey of learning to become one.

That evening Tom and I had a special rededication prayer. We asked God to forgive us for our selfish ways, and also to help us learn to be one and love each other in spite of our difficulties and differences. We recognized that we had a problem, but also knew God had the solution. Together we committed ourselves to study His word, avoid condemning each other, and learn what we needed to do individually to bring harmony into our marriage.

Right away, I began noticing changes in how Tom communicated. He started to express little things he loved and appreciated about me on a

For Better or For ~~Worse~~ Best

daily basis. As for myself, I began to understand him better and learned to respond to him with kindness and respect rather than sharpness. The words of Matthew 7:12, "Therefore all things whatsoever you would that men should do to you, do ye even so to them. ..." began to become our experience. Something so simple and so basic—something that we had both known for years—now became one of the practical solutions we used to redeem our marriage.

That night was the beginning of a new understanding of ourselves and how we had entered the "fatal cycle." We had come together very sincerely, knowing intellectually the two would become one. Yet we didn't really know how that would happen. Up until this point in our young marriage, our habit had been to justify ourselves, blaming each other when misunderstood or crossed, rather than dying to self. Yet in order for any marriage to be happy and healthy, two selfish "me's" must learn how to die so that one "us" can live.

As our relationship continued to grow, we learned to appreciate that each of us brought unique characteristics and perspectives into our marriage that, while beautiful, could separate us at times. Having opposite genders was only the beginning. Like all married couples, we had distinct personalities, upbringings, perspectives, opinions, and idiosyncrasies that played an important role in the make-up of our individuality. Though not wrong in and of themselves, these characteristics tended to magnify the ME in each of us.

When I married Tom, he became my life. Though I had my career, church responsibilities, and outside interests, everything revolved around him. When Tom married me, however, it became evident that I just became another part of his life—an add-on, so to speak—fitting into the gaps that weren't filled. Though we didn't know this about each other initially, once we identified this discrepancy in perspective and adjusted our "thinking," we experienced a new level of harmony and love.

Early in our marriage I was often asked to help organize get-togethers either at church, with friends or Mom's groups. I enjoyed doing these kinds of things so I would usually commit myself without considering my husband's perspective or plans. This is the automatic "me" focus. Learning to think in the "us" focus, I now check with Tom first before

Two "Me's" or One "Us"? (Part I)

committing myself or our family. This has not only helped to prevent me from over-committing, but has resulted in a more harmonious relationship as we have learned to consider each other's plans and desires.

Some women think if they put this principle into practice they will lose their identity or individuality, but this is not true. My enjoyment of organizing get-togethers has not changed, but out of love and respect for Tom, I now seek his input. He not only recognizes if I might be over-committing, but feels free to make suggestions that enhance our get-togethers. We work well together, drawing from each other's strengths.

Becoming one doesn't mean that we lose our individuality—it means losing our selfishness. When two people come together with their strengths and weaknesses, blending the best of two "me's" into a better "us," they are taking part in God's beautiful, perfect plan. This melding is a process, to be sure. As Tom and I so quickly discovered, it means "I" must stop thinking about how my spouse is affecting me, and start thinking about how I can affect "*us*." It is learning that I can let go of **my** way in order to have **our** way, when **our** way will be better for both of us. The experiential reality is that when selfish "me" yields to Christ in order to produce the "us" focus, we **both** experience true fulfillment.

Chapter Five

Two "Me's" or One "Us"? (Part II)

"I don't know why you're getting so upset! I didn't do it on purpose! I think you are just being oversensitive."
Alane and I had just attended the Radiology Department Christmas party, and I had been proud to have my new wife with me. Things started to "go south," however, when we ended up being seated across the dinner table from one of my old girlfriends. We were having pretty good conversation, which Alane was enjoying as well, until Kathy made a sarcastic comment to me that I should have ignored. Instead, I fell into my old pattern of bantering back and forth with the foolishness that used to be so much a part of my old relationship conduct. One thing led to another until I made a pretty poor decision. Picking up a pea, I flicked it at Kathy. Alane was shocked, not only by my conduct, but because the pea ended up going down Kathy's low neck line. Though I didn't mean for that to happen, I did think it was funny.

Disgusted and embarrassed, Alane was quieter than usual for the rest of the evening. When we got into the car I knew why—though I couldn't understand why she was so upset, even hurt.

———•———

It was our first Christmas as a married couple, and I was looking forward to going to Tom's Radiology Department Christmas party. Things were getting better in our marriage. Tom had been more considerate of me, in addition to demonstrating his love and appreciation on a more regular basis. I still had some insecurity around his old friends, however, and was hoping that this party would be kind of a breakthrough for me.

For Better or For ~~Worse~~ Best

I was hoping we would sit with another married couple or someone I knew better, but somehow we ended up with one of Tom's old girlfriends.

"This won't affect our time together," I decided. After all, we were married. The dinner and conversation were going along very nicely, until Kathy made that remark directed at Tom. I was hoping he'd let it go by, but he picked right up on it. The next thing I knew, the two of them were the focus of all at the table.

In an attempt to let Tom know how I felt about his flirtation, I touched his leg and gave it a little squeeze. Ignoring that subtle signal, he kept right on. Then it happened. When Tom flicked that pea at her, it went right into her well-developed bosom. Kathy made the most of it, as Tom and the others nearby all laughed. My instant reaction was far from laughter, however. I was angry, embarrassed, and hurt. I had come hoping for the perfect evening. Now I couldn't wait to get out of there. As the dinner began to wind down, I felt out-of-place and distant from Tom.

"I'm ready to go home," I told him. He asked to be excused, and we left. On the way home, I tried to explain to Tom why what happened had bothered me, but he could only see it as innocent and happenstance. He reassured me that he wasn't interested in Kathy, nor had he tried to aim the pea where it went. I could understand that the pea was an accident, but the flirtatious bantering didn't seem accidental, and it certainly fed Kathy's ego.

Though Tom initially defended his actions, he came back and apologized shortly after we arrived at home.

"When I put myself in your place," he told me, "I can understand why you felt hurt and embarrassed." Tom said he was sorry for not being more sensitive to me in that setting with all his old friends and work associates. He also told me he was proud to be with me at the party, and was glad that I was his wife.

Tom's response really melted my heart. It also confirmed in my mind that our relationship really was improving, and our love was growing. Though there had been some challenges, my dreams of a happy marriage were becoming a reality.

Two "Me's" or One "Us"? (Part II)

Though I listened to what Alane was saying, I reacted with my usual spirit of self-defense, giving her all the reasons why my actions weren't all that bad. Buried beneath the excuses, however, my conscience told me that she was right. My conduct was "me" focused, selfish. I wasn't thinking about my wife. Almost oblivious to her presence, I had slipped into my old flirtatious, single mentality. That night God began opening my eyes to what I now call the "me" focus versus the "us" focus.

As I opened the Word to study the subject, I found that learning to become one is not only possible, *but a biblical expectation. Christ clearly reveals this principle in Matthew 19:4-6:* "Have ye not read, that He which made them at the beginning made them male and female and said, For this cause shall a man leave father and mother, and shall cleave to his wife: and they twain shall be one flesh? Wherefore they are no more twain [two], but one flesh. What therefore God hath joined together, let not man put asunder."

There is a vital action word in these verses that I, like many other husbands, had somehow managed to miss. That word is **cleave**. We are to cleave, or be glued together, to our wives. And as the Bible points out, it is the responsibility of the husband to do the cleaving. This is a much more important point than many men realize. Trouble arises because, when husbands fail to cleave, the natural reaction of the wife is to cling. Men don't like to be clung to if it feels restrictive or possessive. More often than not, the clinging reaction of a wife whose husband isn't cleaving to her causes the husband to distance himself even further. If the husband continues this pattern long enough, the wife eventually detaches herself and survives by developing an attitude that suggests "I don't need you either." As a husband, it is my duty to treat Alane with such love, respect, and tenderness that she is absolutely convinced that I am devoted to her.

This convincing takes more than words—it takes action. Often those loving actions involve very simple things, yet somehow they all add up. God can help us with this, for He knows the little ways to adjust the "me" to strengthen the "us."

Alane and I live about 65 miles from where we do our main shopping. Since we travel a great deal we try to consolidate these trips to

For Better or For ~~Worse~~ Best

town and look for ways to be as efficient as possible with our time. One day I decided to stay in the vehicle to work on correspondence while Alane shopped for groceries, but God had a different plan. Not long after she went into the store, I thought, "Perhaps I should go in and shop with her." Though my first reaction was to justify myself by coming up with reasons for staying in the vehicle, I also knew that Alane would enjoy my company. When I recognized that I was rationalizing and defending the selfish "me" focus, I **chose** by faith to respond to what God was calling to my heart to do. Alane and I had a great time shopping together, and my choice for "us" instead of "me" set a beautiful tone for the rest of the day.

Amos 3:3 asks, "Can two walk together except they be agreed?" There is no other relationship or partnership in this world where these words have more power than in marriage. Alane and I vowed before God and witnesses that we would walk together in sickness and health, prosperity or adversity, for better, for worse, until death would part us. When we found that barriers were forming and our marriage was struggling, we had to stop focusing on each other's problems and ask, "What can I do to make a positive difference?" Alane and I sincerely prayed for God to show us these things at the start of each day, and as we listened for the Holy Spirit's promptings and power, we saw our own marriage transformed by grace. We learned that our marriage would be strengthened as we are first heart-to-heart with God, and then with the one who stands by our side. The more we followed God's promptings and learned to recognize and reject the "me" focus, the more we experienced the joy of becoming "one."

In the end, there were some very simple relationship-building principles that helped us move from the "me" to the "us" focus. No doubt you can benefit from applying these principles as well:

1) **Be determined to be all that you can be for each other**

Notice this does not say to be all you can be for yourself. It means to be all you can be for your spouse. For me personally, that means determining to be:

Two "Me's" or One "Us"? (Part II)

- **The spiritual leader of my home.** This means taking time to seek the Lord through His Word and prayer at the beginning of each day to gain wisdom to guide the affairs of our home. I also ask Him for a loving and sensitive heart to meet the needs of my wife.

- **A good listener.** This means actively listening as my wife speaks, with a true desire to understand her heart rather than merely thinking about what my response will be when she is finished.

- **Honest and transparent.** This means being willing to share my own real life struggles with her—the vulnerability that I may at times feel in my own heart. This also means allowing her to be honest and transparent as we work together for a better "us." For husbands who are not used to being transparent with their wives, this may seem awkward at first. I assure you that you will soon discover rich rewards as you open your heart to her, and the defensive barriers that have built up over time will soon begin to disappear.

- **Healthy and vibrant.** I'm motivated to maintain good health, to exercise and generally take care of myself for her and for us. In a practical sense, this means I keep my hair combed, wear cologne and dress neatly because I care about how I look for my wife, not just for others.

When Tom and I were dating, it wasn't hard to unselfishly put my best foot forward for him. I always wanted to look my best in everything that I did. After the altar, however, it was all too easy to let things "slip." As part of my commitment to him, I have determined to be attractive to him at home as well as in public. I want to be all that I can for him.

Part of being the best I could be also involved learning not to let my emotions control me. When I'm having a "down day" and don't feel like doing anything, I determine that my feelings don't have to affect me and

For Better or For ~~Worse~~ Best

those around me. As I make a choice based on what is right, I have found that my feelings can actually change from gloom to joy. **You see, our feelings follow our thoughts. When we think right thoughts, our feelings will follow.**

---

2) Study to advance the happiness of each other

This seems so natural in the dating or engagement phase of the relationship, but it needs to be consciously carried into the marriage. Ephesians 5:28 says, "So ought men to love their wives as their own bodies. He that loveth his wife loveth himself."

The Lord is very clear on this point! He knows how men tend to love their bodies, how they look at themselves in the mirror. He is telling us to love our wives as we love our own bodies. For me, taking up this challenge means looking for ways to make my wife happy. This is not to be confused with indulgence, which has a very different meaning and effect.

We can learn to shift from the "me" focus to the "us" focus by choosing to take our spouse's perspective into consideration and not just do our own thing or be governed by our own thoughts and desires.

When I was in the "me" focus, looking for ways to make Tom happy didn't come easily. In fact, it took decided effort. Things began to change for me as I went to the Scriptures and prayed to God to gain a better understanding of my role as a wife. And God answered those prayers, by bringing little things to my mind that would make Tom happier. As an added benefit, I, too, was much happier!

Some simple examples of things I could do included making the home an orderly, neat, and peaceful environment. I also began to watch for little things I could do for Tom that would free up his time, such as doing some of his chores, running errands for him, or helping him with a project. When we cultivate a willing and eager heart, there are really limitless things we can do for our spouses to express our love and enhance their happiness. The key is to be truly determined to be all we can be for

Two "Me's" or One "Us"? (Part II)

our spouse and to continually look for ways to make them happy. As we do these things, we will experience a blossoming love.

I know how happy it makes Alane when I make time to really communicate with her. I know it pleases her when I hold her in my arms and tell her how thankful I am to have her for my wife. When I take the responsibility of leadership in our family, so that she isn't left with that burden, I know how happy it makes her. Husbands, our wives need to be able to lean upon our strong yet tender affections. We can pray daily for the Lord to help us identify our wife's needs and to help us meet those needs. We need to seek for wisdom in His Word for ways to increase our sensitivity to improving our wife's genuine happiness.

As Tom and I learned, the more determined we are to do our own thing and have our own way, the more miserable we become and the more discord we will experience in our marriage. The "me" focus always leads to selfishness and unhappiness. On the other side, the more we cooperate with God and submit to His will, the happier we will be and the more self-respect we will have. Free from the bondage of selfishness, we will find ourselves more in love with our spouse and our marriages will truly be heart-to-heart.

Chapter Six

Building a Sure Foundation

Despite the differences we experienced during the early years of our marriage, there were many factors that drew Tom and me together. We were both committed Christians with comparable educational backgrounds. We shared common friends and similar interests. Our personalities were complimentary, and of course, there was a physical attraction as well.

As we learned after our wedding, however, these factors alone are not a sufficient foundation for a successful marriage. There needs to be something underneath the relationship, something more solid that forms the basis of life's decisions. We have learned that there is only one solid, absolute, and immovable foundation for the marriage relationship, and that is the Word of God. It contains all the principles needed to build and nurture a truly heart-to-heart marriage.

If you are not a Christian, you may be thinking, "The Bible won't work for me." But the truth is that whether you are a Christian or not, you are a human being created in the image of God. As God's child, all aspects of your life are dependent on His principles. Many of the sayings or maxims that we have heard all of our lives, even in the secular world, have their basis in biblical truth.

The Golden Rule, which admonishes us to treat others as we wish to be treated, has its foundation in the words of Jesus: "Therefore all things whatsoever ye would that men should do to you, do ye even so to them. ..." (Matthew 7:12).

This simple principle, which has stood the test of time, continues to be very relevant today.

The counsel to "turn the other cheek" and respond to hate with an attitude of love also has biblical roots. "If thine enemy be hungry, give

For Better or For ~~Worse~~ Best

him bread to eat; and if he be thirsty, give him water to drink: for thou shalt heap coals of fire upon his head, and the LORD shall reward thee" *(Proverbs 25:21, 22). In the words of Paul, "Be not overcome of evil, but overcome evil with good" (Romans 12:21). This is another timeless principle that should be applied to marriage. A study of these basic principles will reveal that all of the important rules on how to treat others have their origin in the Word of God. Only the Bible contains the keys to a true and lasting love. If we wish to have a have a happy, peaceful, and fulfilling marriage, then we must base our relationship on the foundation of God's Word.*

In spiritual terms, the "Word" refers not only to Scripture, but to Jesus Himself. John tells us that "in the beginning was the Word, and the Word was with God, and the Word was God ... in Him (the Word) was life; and the life was the light of men" (John 1:1, 4). In addition to being based on Scripture, then, the foundation of a Christian marriage is none other than Jesus. "For other foundation can no man lay than that is laid, which is Jesus Christ" (1 Corinthians 3:11).

———•———

It is not enough to have an intellectual knowledge of Jesus. Knowing Him, and really applying these principles to life and marriage, requires spending time in His Word and in communion with Him.

Though Alane and I wanted a Christian marriage, we fell into this "head knowledge" trap early on. We both believed in Jesus and were actively serving Him. Our lives were very busy doing good things—so busy, in fact, that we had no time for God. Between church functions, work-related activities, social functions and maintaining friendships, we were going to bed late and finding it hard to get up. Our morning routine consisted of a quick prayer at best, reading a devotional page, and breakfast on the run. This inevitable result was no vital connection with Christ and no assimilation of His Word. Though we knew our Bibles and could answer religious questions correctly, Jesus and His living Word were not the source and guide for our actual day-to-day lives. No wonder we struggled to conquer the irritation and anxiety in our lives. Instead of yielding to the direct management of the Holy Spirit, we were managing ourselves.

Building a Sure Foundation

After we truly made God's Word the foundation of our marriage, little things in life that might have caused a conflict at one point in our marriage no longer do. Such small, seemingly insignificant interactions make up the sum of our daily lives—and how we handle them reflects whether or not we are truly choosing to have Christ and His Word as our sure foundation.

Today we have an agreement: if we don't see eye to eye on something, we share our perspectives with each other. If this step doesn't bring unity, we individually go to the Bible, searching for applicable principles and what God has to say on the subject. We don't study to prove our point, but to know what is right and best. After studying the issue, we come together to discuss it, sharing what we have learned. This practice of letting God be the authority in all things has resulted in a more peaceful, happy, and harmonious marriage.

Long before Alane and I met, I memorized James 1:19: "Let every man be swift to hear, slow to speak, slow to wrath." But though I knew this verse by heart, I had not allowed it to make a practical impact on my communication with Alane. I wasn't swift to hear; I was swift to speak. I wasn't slow to wrath; I was quick to become irritated.

When I began to see the difference between what I professed and my actions towards Alane, I was led to establish a better connection with God and yield myself to His will. I learned that experiencing a real need for a Savior was a very different experience from simply "saying" that I loved Jesus. I determined to make time for communion with God a priority in my life.

Together, Alane and I started seeking Christ first in the day (Matthew 6:33). We wanted to start each morning in communion with God. We also made the decision to go to bed earlier so we could wake up sooner. Some of our lifestyle choices weren't compatible with our decision to live by the principles of God's Word or make Jesus Master of our lives, so we changed them as well.

For Better or For ~~Worse~~ Best

The changes we made have truly impacted our lives. Our religion is not just a set of theoretical beliefs. Neither is it limited to one day a week. By God's grace, Christ and His Word have truly become the basis of our lives. This experience continues to grow deeper and is literally what gets us up in the morning, why we live the way we do, and how we obtain the power to succeed. And the good news is that regardless of where your marriage is right now, you can have this experience too.

Chapter Seven

An Enduring Commitment

Since that first year of our marriage when Tom and I had to make so many adjustments, we have become acquainted with many couples who separated or eventually divorced. One of the reasons such couples often give for the rift in their marriage is that there is "no love" or "nothing left" in their relationship.

There is something left, however. There is a marriage pledge, a vow, a covenant for life. There is also an enduring commitment that is not to be broken "till death do us part"! It is not optional or conditional—it is a binding contract under God between a husband and wife. This commitment is a safeguard to keep our changeable emotions from suggesting divorce as an option.

Marriage is not a proposition where each spouse gives fifty percent. God tells us in Philippians 2:3 that we should each esteem the other better than ourselves. We must be willing to give all—yes, 100%—because that's what He did for us. Instead of demanding that your spouse fulfill their marriage vows to you, focus on demonstrating your commitment to them. Jesus exemplified this principle for us, in that "while we were yet sinners, He died for us" (Romans 5:8). As a result, "We love Him because He first loved us." (1 John 4:19) This principle will prove effective in winning the heart of our spouse as well.

It is amazing what we can tolerate from a co-worker, acquaintance, or even a stranger—when we have so little tolerance for our spouse, the one we said we loved above all others and wanted to spend the rest of our life with. Many people put tremendous effort into their education, careers, and future security, while exerting very little effort towards building a successful marriage relationship. It appears that marriage has very little priority in our actual, day-to-day lives. This paradox is not only amazing, but tragic.

For Better or For ~~Worse~~ Best

Even if think you have no feeling left for your spouse, or that there is no hope, love can be rekindled. Feelings can change, misunderstandings can be worked through, walls can be broken down, and hurts can be healed.

The key thing to remember is that, in addition to the fact that thoughts follow feelings, feelings also follow thoughts. If you think disparaging and hopeless thoughts about your relationship, you will invariably be cultivating hopeless and disparaging feelings. If, on the other hand, you choose to think of the positive attributes your spouse possesses and to view your relationship with hope, your feelings toward your spouse will begin to change. Love "beareth all things, believeth all things, hopeth all things, endureth all things" (1 Corinthians 13:7).

Ask God to caution you when your thoughts are tending in a negative direction. Then cooperate with His guidance to experience the power of this verse in your marriage.

One day, I received a call from a man who had seen our marriage program on 3ABN television. He had already signed divorce papers, but when he saw the program he was convicted to try one more time. I suggested that he ask his wife, who was living in another state, if she would be willing to have a 3-way phone conversation. She agreed, and through the grace of God and a willingness of both spouses to cooperate, a positive change took place. Before we ended the call with prayer, the husband agreed to meet his wife. Together, they burned the divorce papers and renewed their marriage commitment.

This was a miracle of God, for He alone empowers us to keep our commitments. Jesus is the same miracle worker today as He was when He walked on this earth. He is the one who can give you the strength, desire, and willingness to make your commitment endure.

Regardless of the current status of your relationship—whether you have a solid, living commitment or one that is weak and vacillating—that commitment can be more enduring through cooperation with God's basic plan for marriage.

As you seek to follow this plan, the first step is to **remember the vows** you made as husband and wife. Read them to each other again,

An Enduring Commitment

recommitting yourselves anew to the pledge you made on your wedding day. Walk down "memory lane" with your spouse, reflecting on what brought you together and how God has blessed you. If you don't feel like reminiscing, prayerfully move forward in faith and do it anyway. God will bless your efforts. As you contemplate the positive aspects of what each of you bring to the marriage, your appreciation for each other will increase and your marriage commitment will strengthen.

Second, **seek the Lord**. Be willing to spend time in prayer and reflect on how you are upholding your side of the commitment. Be open to God's insights into what may be weakening your commitment and how you can strengthen your marriage.

Third, **evaluate and commit**. As a couple, discuss where your commitment has weakened. Then share what you are willing to change, by God's grace, in order to strengthen it. Ask your spouse if there is anything you need to change. Be sensitive here! This is not intended to turn into a negative, critical, faultfinding session, but rather an open exchange of mutual "us"-focused conversation. This kind of communication should end in a sense of increased camaraderie and a sincere desire to work together. This step is powerful, especially if both parties are truly willing to work together.

Lastly, **don't lose hope**! If you think your marriage is too fractured, your communication too painful, and your hope is nearly gone, don't give up! Surrender yourself unreservedly to Christ. He will teach you how to love when you feel unloved, how to give when you get nothing in return.

We saw these concepts beautifully illustrated in one family. Turning from God, the husband had been caught in worldly addictions and vices. As she saw her husband and the father of her children drifting farther and farther away, the wife responded with natural human hurt, anger, and bitterness. In desperation she poured out her broken heart to God, seeking Him for answers, and then surrendered herself completely to Him. Once she reached the point where she was fully willing to accept God's leading, He gave her the solution. And it was based on what she was to do, not her husband. She determined that she and her children

For Better or For ~~Worse~~ Best

would give daddy the only heaven he might ever experience. *God poured the gift of heaven-born love into her heart, and it flowed out to her ill-tempered, discontented husband. Though she would not compromise her faith, she did everything she could to create a little bit of heaven at home for him.*

Months later, her husband returned to his senses and to the Lord. His heart returned to his wife, and he became the man God wanted him to be. He came back, he said, because he had seen real Christianity displayed—in a way he had never seen it before. As he witnessed the self-sacrificing love of his wife, it kindled a desire within his heart which eventually led him back to God.

If your spouse has wandered far from God, do not give up hope! Perhaps you will have the opportunity to fulfill the words of inspiration, "For what knowest thou, O wife, whether thou shalt save thy husband? Or how knowest thou, O man, whether thou shalt save thy wife?" (1 Corinthians 7:16).

Though it is certainly ideal for both partners to recognize their spiritual need and surrender to the life-changing power of Christ, a powerful difference can be made even if only one is willing.

Early on in our marriage, Alane and I had quite a few hurts and issues to work through. Despite the trials of adjustment, however, we both knew that God had brought us together. Though we didn't understand each other at times, we were committed to God and each other through vows that did not allow us to give up. **Divorce was not an option.** We had already predetermined that, so we didn't even allow our minds to go down that road. We would stay in our marriage no matter what trials or difficulties might come our way. There were only two things that could have dissolved our marriage: death, or fornication as defined by Jesus in Matthew 19:9.

Alane and I also cherish the foundation of an enduring marriage commitment laid for us by our parents' example. During our most painful and difficult times, the influence of our parents' example became evident to us, as divorce never entered our minds. During those difficult moments, commitment was the glue that kept our marriage

An Enduring Commitment

together. Sometimes simply verbalizing that commitment helped bring reconciliation between us.

If you find yourself wavering in your marriage commitment, perhaps now would be a good time to repeat your vow to love each other in sickness and in health, prosperity and adversity, for richer or poorer, better or worse, forsaking all others till death "do us part." Unfortunately, many marriage partners have fallen into the trap of transposing those vows to read "I promise to love, honor, comfort, and cherish—until ... you yell at me, lie to me, hurt my feelings, spend all my money, look at other women, or fail to keep a clean house." That is not what the marriage vow said, however. Worse yet, it is disastrous thinking which—if left unchecked—will lead to deadly thoughts that divide and conquer commitment, such as:

- "He doesn't really care for me. I'd be better off without him."
- "She never keeps the house clean. I'm not going to live in this mess."
- "He lies to me all the time. I just can't trust him."
- "She is the biggest airhead I know. I'm not going to take her unreasonableness."
- "He yells at me all the time. I'm not going to spend the rest of my life listening to him scream at me."
- "She undermines my authority. I'm not going to take it anymore."
- "He doesn't spend any time with the kids. I might as well be a single parent."
- "She spends my money like it grows on trees. I'm not going to work myself to death. I need to get ahead for myself."
- "We don't get along anymore. We would be better off going our separate ways."
- "We don't have any common interests. We would be better off doing our own thing."
- "He looks at other women all the time. I think he's having an affair."

For Better or For ~~Worse~~ Best

- "She's always nagging me. I'm not going to put up with it any longer."

Such thoughts are extremely dangerous, since once we let them into our minds they become our **reality**. Soon we begin to see everything in that light, and before long we are responding with drastic measures in order to "cope."

One of my greatest struggles in the early part of our marriage was controlling my thoughts when things didn't go the way I thought they should. I would replay a situation in my mind over and over again, each time picking up momentum until my emotions were stirred up and my feelings were agitated or hurt. Little things grew into big things and then using these thoughts as a springboard, the devil was right there to prompt me to wonder if my husband really did love me.

Thankfully, God showed me that I had to come face to face with this particular area of my life in order to preserve our enduring commitment. I realized that my mind was capable of swinging from one extreme to another—from thinking about happy times together to dwelling on a terrible disappointment or a misunderstanding. This would then result in a negative reaction toward Tom that in reality was my problem, not his.

When I started facing and then dealing with my problem of uncontrolled thoughts, I began to form the habit of looking for the good and lovely which were already there but had become obscured by my own selfishness. As I started thinking of all the nice things Tom did for me, instead of focusing on what he didn't do, my entire outlook began to change and we both saw tremendous growth in our marriage.

Paul was talking about this powerful principle of thought control when he wrote, "Finally brethren, whatsoever things are true, whatsoever things are honest, whatsoever things are just, whatsoever things are pure, whatsoever things are lovely, whatsoever things are of a good report, if there be any virtue, and if there be any praise, **think on these things**" (Philippians 4:8). If we would individually put this simple biblical principle into practice in our daily lives, we would have an "enduring commitment" and a dramatic improvement in the peace, happiness, and contentment in our marriages.

Chapter Eight
Effective Communication

When Tom and I were engaged we looked for every opportunity we could find to talk, especially since we worked different shifts. I recall many evenings spent eagerly anticipating Tom's break time, knowing that he would call for ten minutes. We took advantage of every opportunity to hear each other's voice, to share an experience, express our love and appreciation, or just to say, "I'm missing you." We loved to make time for each other and to talk. But after we were married our communication began to deteriorate.

I remember coming home from work one evening during our first year of marriage. I was tired and had a lot on my mind. Alane met me at the door and wanted to talk, but I let her know I was busy and didn't have time. Then the phone rang and Alane answered. It was my best friend and I took the call, which resulted in a lively thirty-minute conversation. So lively and animated, in fact, that Alane couln't wait to hear what was so fascinating!

"What did he have to say?" she asked when I hung up the phone.

"Oh, nothing," I replied, with no consideration for how she might feel. This flippant response communicated some very powerful—though unintentional—messages to my wife: not only am I too tired to talk to you, but I've got time for my friend; and after spending thirty minutes with him, I still don't have time to talk with you. I shut her out on both ends of the phone call. That was not effective communication!

The Lord used Alane's silence to show me how terrible it was to treat my wife this way, even though I had not done so intentionally. The message I was communicating to the woman I had vowed to love

For Better or For ~~Worse~~ Best

and cherish really hit me. What an awakening! Many of us need to pay attention to the type of communication and expressiveness we use in talking with co-workers, friends, and fellow church members, comparing it to the communication we have with our own spouse.

Hebrews 13:16 is a very encouraging Bible verse that is especially appropriate for most men: "To communicate forget not, for with such sacrifices God is well pleased." Though we may not always feel like taking time to communicate with our spouse, God is well pleased with whatever "sacrifice" we make to communicate well.

Making communication a priority will produce a significant difference in our marriage. Good communication builds solid relationships. The more we commune with God, the closer our bond and the more in tune we are with Him. The same is true in our marriages—the more effectively we communicate, the closer we are. Like Tom and I, most couples don't have much trouble communicating during their dating and engagement. It is natural to be thinking of the other person and the things we want to share with them. But though not intentional, something often happens when the honeymoon phase is over—and that something is not good! Following are several ways to promote effective communication in our marriage.

#1 Make (and take) time for consistent communication

Most of us seem to find time for things that we feel are important. For married couples, communication should be one of those things. Make time in your schedule to communicate with your spouse, then stick with your commitment as planned.

When I made this commitment to have daily communication with Alane, I began with a short time—20-30 minutes. During this time, I committed to listening intently to her needs. I wanted to communicate that she was important to me and that I sincerely wanted to know what was on her heart.

It's especially important for stay-at-home moms, who may become weary of communicating on a child's level during the day, to know that

Effective Communication

their spouse really cares and does want to listen. By the end of a day, they long for the understanding of their husband and communication on an adult level.

Whether your wife is at home or not, women have an intense need for heart level communication and mutual understanding. Don't overlook this important aspect for building effective communication.

The key is to plan the time, guard it, then make it a mutually fulfilling experience. Don't wait until you think you will have more time. That time will never come. And remember, this communication time is not a time to present your "honey do" list, nor a time to complain or nag, or use generic, short answers such as, "good," "okay," "whatever you want," "uh-huh," etc. Both parties must be fully engaged in the conversation and not thinking about other things. It needs to be a true two-way dialog with both husband and wife participating. You want this to be a time you look forward to, not dread. As you begin this talk time together, be sure to filter your words, choosing them carefully, and blend positive appreciation with the necessary problem solving topics.

#2 **Listen with a heart to understand**

Effective communication means listening with a heart to hear and understand what the other person intends to communicate. It doesn't mean hearing just enough to begin thinking about a response before your spouse has finished their thought! To really listen, I need to tune into the **heart** of my wife and process what she is saying *before* I respond. Often it helps to communicate back to her what I think she is trying to say. I have found the prayer in 1 Kings 3:9 to be helpful in this regard: "Give therefore thy servant an understanding heart."

Our natural human tendency is to want others to understand us first before we bother to understand them. We also tend to defend self, thinking, "I know what you're going to say before you are finished speaking, therefore I can interrupt you with my response." I used to interrupt Alane by saying things like "but you don't understand" or "I know what you're thinking." In either case I was not giving her

For Better or For ~~Worse~~ Best

the courtesy of completing her thoughts. The wise man pointedly addressed this human tendency to be defensive and interruptive, writing that "he that answereth a matter before he heareth it, it is folly and shame unto him" (Proverbs 18:13).

Listening with a heart to understand what the other is saying doesn't necessarily mean we agree with them. What it does mean is that we are committed to understanding their perspective before we respond. Understanding another's perspective also means seeking to understand what a person is **trying** to say, even though they may be having difficulty expressing it.

When this desire to understand each other is evident in our communication, barriers are broken down, and misunderstandings and arguments are avoided. Your hearts will be drawn together as you seek to jointly understand an issue, and often you will gain a different perspective in the process. I have realized that it means more to Alane to know that I understand her, than that I agree with her. One of the benefits of developing good listening skills is that understanding and agreement come so much more easily. If we will first listen to the still, small voice of the Holy Spirit calling to our conscience we will become better listeners when communicating with our spouses.

#3 Allow for differences of opinion and perspective

When I think of an opinionated person, I think of someone who is not only adamant about their view, but also dislikes it when others think differently. If this is how we relate in our marriage, we're in trouble. It is OK to have differing opinions and perspectives on a subject, as long as they don't conflict with Bible principle. In fact, many arguments and misunderstandings could be avoided if we are willing to allow for differences.

The fact that a wife differs in opinion from her husband does not mean she is threatening his authority or position. Women need the freedom to express their differing viewpoints, and the sooner that is allowed, the sooner the couple can be in harmony on the more important matters. Effective communication allows for differences of opinion and perspective. All of us analyze things differently. We remember

Effective Communication

things differently. We don't have to always see things the same or think the same in every situation.

It is important to understand the distinction between a difference of opinion or perspective and a difference of principle. Principle is always exacting and is to be the governing agency underlying all our decisions and practices. It should be our purpose as a couple to find agreement on principle. For example, Ephesians 6:1, "Children, obey your parents in the Lord," is a principle from God's Word, so it is important to be in agreement on this point. One parent cannot reasonably say, "Our child does not need to obey."

Early in our marriage we found ourselves debating over who was right; each bringing up facts to prove it. But, we weren't happy, as no one will be when they have to argue their point. Once we realized what was happening (recognizing the big "ME" that never wants to be wrong) we learned to glean from each other's perspective. As a result, both of us gained a broader understanding of the other and our conversations became much more pleasant.

#4 Express appreciation

Expressing appreciation for each other is another form of effective communication. Unfortunately, it is human nature to express what we don't like rather than to voice what we do. When negativity becomes the norm in our communication, we prepare the way not only for a communication breakdown, but also a relationship breakdown. How long has it been since we said:

- *"Thank you for the great dinner!" rather than, "What's for dessert?"*
- *"Thank you for taking time for the kids tonight. I can tell they really enjoyed their time with you," rather than, "It's about time you spent some time with the kids. They hardly even know who you are anymore."*
- *"I appreciate that you did the dishes," instead of, "I'm tired of coming home and finding things such a mess."*

For Better or For ~~Worse~~ Best

More good is done by simple, honest words of appreciation and encouragement than by expressing our unhappiness, disagreement or displeasure. Positive statements will do more to motivate change than exaggerations, overstatements, and isolated examples. Learn to state less-than-positive things in the best possible light. For example, instead of saying, "My husband is a terrible mechanic," say, "Being a mechanic is not one of my husband's strengths."

Many husbands have high expectations of their wives, but very little appreciation for what they do. To further complicate this problem, they may also have a very low expectation of what they as a husband can do to brighten, lighten, and cheer her day. The good news is that, under the influence of the Holy Spirit, this mindset can be changed.

Husbands, begin praying today that God will open your heart and help you to express appreciation for your wife. I have learned by experience that an appreciative husband has a much happier wife. I am genuinely thankful for what Alane does, and express my appreciation daily. I kiss her at each meal as an expression of my love and appreciation for being with her and for her love to me in preparing and serving our meals. I express appreciation for the support she is to me in our ministry. I tell her how nice she looks and how much it means to me that she takes care of herself. I tell her she's the love of my life and there is no one else I'd rather be with. If you do not regularly express appreciation for your wife, I invite you to give it a try. The difference appreciation can make in a relationship is simply amazing!

#5 Be sensitive to non-verbal communication

Did you realize that far more communication happens non-verbally than verbally? We need to pay close attention to this part of our daily communication! Nonverbal communication is often more powerful than words, both in the positive and negative sense. We may look the other way when our spouse is saying something we don't want to hear. This disconnect from the conversation only creates a wider gap in our communication and in our hearts. We can break this cycle by being sensitive

Effective Communication

to our responses, choosing to listen with a heart and desire to understand, and looking at our spouse with respect rather than disaffection or disapproval.

One evening when our family was enjoying some good "talk time," I decided to be vulnerable and ask if there were any areas in which my family felt I had room for improvement. One of my children took the opportunity to point out when I didn't like something or things seemed to be going wrong, I would "wrinkle" my forehead. After discussing the matter, I gave them all permission to respectfully let me know the next time this happened.

"But, Father, that's not a good time to tell you that you have a wrinkled forehead," one of my children replied. I assured them all that I wanted to deal with this strong non-verbal communication and that by God's grace I would respond to the Holy Spirit when my family reminded me of it.

A few days later a situation arose where the much-discussed wrinkled forehead surfaced. One of my children brought it to my attention. Though I didn't like hearing about it at the moment, the Holy Spirit reminded me of my desire to deal with this negative form of communication. With God's help, I responded positively to the His promptings—and to my daughter. Though this form of nonverbal communication rarely occurs anymore, I now usually recognize when it does—and deal with it at the source—in my thinking.

When used to express love or appreciation, nonverbal communication can bring a new sparkle into the marriage relationship. A nice smile, which goes a long way towards building love and deepening communication, is a good example of this. I have made it a habit to smile often at Tom, as well as our children, and this little choice has made a huge impact in our family. Not only that, I feel better when I smile. Our feelings are reflected in our actions and our actions reflect on our feelings. I now receive many spontaneous smiles from Tom, even when his mind appears to be somewhere else.

For Better or For ~~Worse~~ Best

Recently, when Tom and I were walking through a very congested airport, I ended up ahead of him. When I turned around to look for him, he gave me a big grin—which brought a smile to my face. I immediately became aware that the people around us noticed our nonverbal communication, and I could tell by their expressions they liked what they saw. It is amazing how one little smile can affect your day and that of others, as well!

Tom's office used to be in our bedroom, and sometimes I would go sit on the bed behind him and watch him work. Sensing my gaze, he often turned around and asked me if I needed anything or if everything was OK.

"Everything is fine," I would reassure him. "I don't need anything."

"Don't you have anything to do?" he would ask me then.

"Of course there is," I responded. "I always have something to do, but I just felt like being with you for a few minutes."

At first that sort of response used to make Tom feel funny, but now he loves it and understands that I just want to be near him. This form of nonverbal communication has been very positive in our marriage and has drawn us closer, making the better best.

Other positive nonverbal expressions are winking, love notes left in unexpected places, taking our spouse's hand, or a spontaneous hug. Don't wait until you feel like doing these things before actually doing them. As you communicate in these positive nonverbal ways, you will begin to see the difference it makes, not only in your spouse's heart but in your own. Create your own special, intimate, and effective, nonverbal forms of communication, and your love and respect for one another will blossom and grow.

#6 Stay on the topic

As simple as it may seem, staying on the topic of discussion until it is understood and resolved is paramount in good communication. When an important conversation is started, then one person brings up a separate but somewhat-related issue, the second issue often derails the original conversation, taking it down a negative track. Alane calls this "freight training" because the conversation starts getting loaded

Effective Communication

with irrelevant freight until the current topic stalls from the overload of past issues. When such additional baggage is brought into a conversation, confusion and disagreements arise.

This tends to happen when there has not been regular communication. Past issues that have been suppressed come out once communication opens up.

In our marriage, I was more guilty of "freight training" than Tom. I was also usually the one who felt hurt when the conversation turned sour. To deal with this communication breaker in our marriage, we made an agreement to respectfully remind one another whenever a conversation began moving off topic. By addressing one topic with a desire to understand each other, then expressing ourselves in the most positive way, we have been able to reach workable solutions and strengthen our relationship. As we have learned, it is better to deal with one thing at a time.

#7 Maintain honesty and integrity

Honesty and integrity are two very powerful elements of effective communication. Though we live in a society that flaunts (and even glamorizes) dishonesty, this selfish, "me"-focused indulgence has only increased the heartache of broken families. The old adage "Honesty is the best policy" is still true today.

I once received a call from a man asking for prayerful input on a decision he faced. For some time, he had been emotionally involved with a woman besides his wife. Now, under the constraining power of the Holy Spirit, he had turned away from this secret relationship. He was convinced that he should confess his conduct to his wife, but feared that this confession—with the hurt and betrayal it entailed—would cause his wife to distrust him.

"I believe your conviction to be transparent with your wife is from the Lord," I assured him. "Your honesty should build her trust, not destroy it." I explained that it was this kind of honesty that would give her the ability to believe in him again. This repentance and confession would solve the mystery in her mind of why he had been distant

For Better or For ~~Worse~~ Best

from her, for she was no doubt intuitively aware that something was wrong. The man thanked me for confirming what he already knew he must do, and for encouraging him to move beyond the devil's lies and fears.

What a delight to see this couple months later at a marriage seminar we were conducting. They were radiant and shared their experience of how God had blessed the husband's honesty by preparing his wife's heart for what the husband had had to confess. With God's help, she did not react with hurt or anger to what her husband shared about his vulnerability. While an emotional response would have been normal, such a reaction would have also discouraged his openness, causing him to retreat into silence or lack of transparency.

She wisely recognized that, when her husband was willing to humbly confess what he had done and seek forgiveness, it was an indication he truly wanted to change and needed her help. By honestly admitting he made a mistake and desiring to have nothing to do with his former choices or habits, he became ready to face himself. He needed forgiveness, encouragement, and help to find victory to overcome temptations. By being tenderhearted and forgiving, she was a true "help meet." She had become his accountability partner, and with God's help she was strengthening and encouraging his commitment.

If you recognize the Holy Spirit calling to your heart about an honesty issue, don't hide and don't cover it up. Be honest. If you are struggling with Internet pornography, don't sell your soul for something that cheap. Honestly deal with the heart issues with God and your wife. The promise is, "Then will I sprinkle clean water upon you, and ye shall be clean: from all your filthiness, and all your idols, will I cleanse you. A new heart also will I give you, and a new Spirit will I put within you, and I will take away the stony heart out of your flesh, and I will give you a heart of flesh. And I will put My Spirit within you, and cause you to walk in My statutes, and ye shall keep My judgments and do them" (Ezekiel 36:25-27). What a powerful promise that is!

Honesty should also extend to the "little things" such as nonverbal responses. Early in our marriage, I often felt that Tom misunderstood or

Effective Communication

hurt me. When he would ask how I was doing, I didn't want to be truthful, so I would often say, "I am fine!"

I wanted Tom to recognize my need without me having to tell him; for him to seek me out and really tune in to my heart. My answer, however, usually ended our conversation rather than drawing the desired response from him. This led me to even greater frustration and hurt. I could have avoided much of this if I had been honest with Tom about how I was feeling, rather than trying to cover it up and hope he would perceive my need.

Honesty has had a powerful impact on our relationship as husband and wife. We have found it to be essential to effective communication. Even if what we have to say is not always pleasant or positive, being truthful and forthright with our spouse shows a level of trust that is willing to be vulnerable. Being honest consistently almost guarantees that a marriage will not fall into the destructive "can't trust him" or "can't trust her" syndrome which inevitably leads to stressful communication or worse yet, no communication at all.

As we learn to share our thoughts and hearts using the strategies and communication tools above, we will find ourselves falling more deeply in love. We will discover the joys of deep, honest, vulnerable communication, which will bind our hearts as one. We will be more perceptive of one another's needs, seek more time to talk, share our heart more freely, and be drawn closer to each other. Don't wait for your spouse. Begin being completely and unreservedly honest today and see for yourself the difference it will make in your marriage.

Chapter Nine

Communication Breakers

While we like to focus on positive principles, it is also important to identify the culprits that undermine effective communication. Colossians 4:6, which counsels us to "let your speech be always with grace. ..." is a good verse to keep in mind when considering the seven sure-fire communication breakers described below:

Communication Breaker #1: Making absolute statements

It is our natural tendency to exaggerate certain situations in order to make our point clear or forceful. Often we do this without realizing it by using these two common phrases, "You always ..." or "You never ..." Such words, which do not represent reality, lead conversations in a negative direction, ending in a communication breakdown rather than resolution and harmony.

Early in our marriage we sometimes found ourselves using some very hurtful, negative words in our communication. As we explored why our conversations went awry we were able to identify absolute statements as the trigger points that inevitably led us down the path of communication breakdown. Once we identified these points we determined to make the necessary changes to more accurately represent a situation. We were tired of the miscommunication, frustration, and hurt that we experienced as a result of these ill-chosen words.

Alane and I have agreed that any time one of us uses an absolute term, the other can respectfully ask if that is really what we meant to say. This call to accountability allows us to restate our thoughts more accurately, then move on gracefully. We have found eliminating absolute terms to be very helpful in fostering positive communication.

Communication Breaker #2: Bringing up the past

We once counseled a couple who couldn't agree on anything—except that they hadn't agreed on anything for years! We soon discovered that a large part of their very serious communication problem was due to their habit of repeatedly bringing up the past.

During our first counseling session, they were well into their story when we suggested that we all take a break.

"We enjoy taking an evening walk and talk together," I told them, mentioning that it would probably be a good thing for them as well. During the walk, we suggested they agree to limit their communication to what attracted them to each other in the beginning and what they appreciated about each other.

"We won't be able to think of anything positive," they quickly informed us. "It has been so long since we had those kinds of thoughts!"

"If you ask God for help and are willing to cooperate, He will remind you of your positive times," we assured them. Then we sent them down the road one way, and prayed as we walked the other direction.

We wish you could have seen their faces when we met up with them again. Smiling and happy, they said they had not enjoyed communicating like that in over ten years. This couple experienced a great change in their lives and God helped them restore their marriage because they chose to focus on positives from the past instead of the negative.

―――――――――●―――――――――

Bringing up the past is such a part of our human nature that it's almost automatic—especially if we are trying to convince someone that our perspective is right. Dredging up negative experiences, attitudes, or words to support present issues is harmful to a marriage. This tactic almost always derails conversations, resulting in additional frustration, misunderstanding, and hurt. Meanwhile, the original issue remains unresolved.

When Tom and I understood the damaging effects of this type of communication, we made an agreement that neither of us would bring up the past to support, justify, or defend ourselves. We also agreed that if

Communication Breakers

one of us slips, rather than becoming defensive, the other can simply voice a reminder that we made an agreement not to bring up the past. What a blessing this habit has been, since it makes our communication flow more easily and positively.

Communication Breaker #3: Loudness, screaming, yelling, or muttering

Some people seem to think that the louder something is said, the more chance there is that the message will finally "get through." Others always want to "have the last word." When communication breaks down, they walk away but keep muttering half-audible words of disgust.

If they could watch a video of themselves yelling, screaming, or muttering, most couples would be appalled. Such communication is a lose-lose proposition. It never enlightens anyone, doesn't bring a better understanding of the subject, and never solves disagreements. Yelling does cause people to lose credibility and respect for each other. It also reinforces the "ME" focus and makes the "yeller" feel out-of-control.

———◆———

There are many scriptures that discuss the power of the tongue for both good and evil. Following are just a few that have transformed our communication:

- "A soft answer turneth away wrath, but grievous words stir up anger" (Proverbs 15:1).
- "Death and life are in the power of the tongue" (Proverbs 18:21).
- "Whoso keepeth his mouth and his tongue keepeth his soul from troubles" (Proverbs 21:23).

Other approaches that have been helpful during times of difficulty in our marriage include:

- Repeating that "we" were not the enemy, that the devil and self are the real enemies of good communication and good relationships—and that we, as a couple, should be allies against these common foes.

For Better or For ~~Worse~~ Best

- Making a personal commitment to avoid destructive means of expression.
- Asking God to show us when emotions are rising, so that we can choose to let Him subdue our hearts, giving us the right words to speak and a right spirit in their delivery.

If you implement these, you will find that not only will your spouse have more respect for what you have to say, but you will have more self-dignity as well. It is a win-win situation—always!

Communication Breaker #4: Driving on ice

If you've ever traveled on icy roads, you know what a nerve-wracking experience it can be. When accidents have been seen, others around you are sliding into the median or ditch, it's natural for the driver to focus straight ahead, driving silently with a great deal of concentration. Problems arise, however, when one spouse (usually the husband) acts like they are "driving on ice" when really they are sitting at the kitchen table, on the front porch, or in their living room recliner. The wife tries to initiate a conversation, but the man looks straight ahead, silently, as though in a great deal of concentration. Occasionally (when prompted), he grunts short responses that reveal his true disinterest.

When the same man is talking about golf, fishing, or some other hobby with a good friend, the scene is much different. Even when behind the wheel, the husband and a good friend seated in the front seat next to him may have such an animated conversation that their wives (in the back seat) worry if they will run off the road!

The good news is that, even after marriage, spouses can have such animated conversations with each other. It's all about our choice—a choice between the selfish "me" focus or the focus on "us." If you pray about your attitude toward communicating with your spouse, then put a plan into action, you will be amazed at how much more pleasant travel time can be with the love of your life!

Communication Breakers

Tom and I can easily identify with this common communication barrier because it was a frequent occurrence early in our marriage. As we drove to and from work Tom would be very focused and intent on his driving, rarely talking to or looking at me. This, despite the fact that, before we got married, he looked over at me often and never lacked for something to say.

When the honeymoon was over, however, we would make the 30-40 minute morning drive to work in silence and return home the same way. One morning when I asked Tom why he never talked to me on the way to work, he replied without hesitation that he wasn't a morning person. I eventually asked why he didn't talk to me during the afternoon commute either. This time he wasn't as quick with his answer but he eventually said, "I've just got a lot on my mind and I'm tired."

It was a different story when one of Tom's friends rode with us, however. Then he would engage in an energetic conversation. This happened frequently enough that I began to wonder what was wrong with me. Why didn't he like to talk to me? Why didn't he share his thoughts with me the way he did with his buddies? I began to feel insecure and to question his love.

I share these thoughts and feelings not because they were right, but because they are typical. Also, once such thoughts begin they bring corresponding responses that result in further separation. We may respond to our spouse with sarcasm or indifference (in the same way we think that our husband is intentionally treating us). In most cases, however, our spouse is unaware they are doing anything wrong or hurtful. Their action doesn't represent a lack of love, but rather a lack of the "us" focus on their part.

One day I shared with Tom how I felt in the most positive, matter-of-fact way I knew how. I was amazed to discover that he hadn't even realized how I felt about the way he communicated with me versus how he communicated with his friends. He understood what I was saying, and felt bad he been communicating to me I was less important to him than his friend. I let him know I would like to hear what he was thinking, even if he thought it might not be interesting to me.

This conversation was a turning point in deepening our communication, and for many years now he no longer "drives on ice."

For Better or For ~~Worse~~ Best

Communication Breaker #5: Nodding off during a "talk"

When a husband or wife falls asleep during what (to the other) seemed like an important conversation, it leaves the awake party questioning the value of their words! This is one of the reasons why we don't use bedtime as our regular "talk time." Though the moments just after going to bed might seem like a good time to open up and share what is on your heart, your spouse may be so tired that he or she is likely to fall asleep—leaving the impression that what we have to say is not important or they don't really care. Neither of these conclusions is usually accurate, and if believed, only cause more stress in communication.

———•———

If the bedroom is the only place where you have privacy in your home, try sitting up in bed while you communicate, instead of lying down. If you have begun a deep conversation with your spouse but find that you really are too tired to continue, politely ask if the discussion can continue in the morning. This is a simple courtesy, but it is a whole lot better than nodding off when your spouse is trying to share the thoughts of their heart!

Communication Breaker #6: Inappropriate laughter and tears

When Alane and I were going through a very difficult time in our early marriage, I would sometimes talk very seriously and intensely about something I felt was extremely important for her to understand. Seemingly out of nowhere she would start giggling. I couldn't understand this response.

"Why are you laughing?" I would ask. "I am very serious about this." This usually caused her to giggle harder, irritating me even more. Needless to say, this was a real communication breaker for us. Later, when I came to understand that Alane's giggling was a nervous response to the intense conversations, my eyes became opened to the real cause of her inappropriate laughter.

———•———

As a gift from God, tears certainly have their place in healthy communication. If your tears are motivated by a realization that you have

Communication Breakers

been wrong and it breaks your heart to see your fault, they are acceptable and can actually strengthen your relationship. Used inappropriately, however, tears can become a communication breaker. Tears are God-given, but can also be misused in communication, turned on and off for not-so-honorable purposes. The issue is not the tears themselves, but whether the tears needlessly break communication and hinder resolving our differences. A man changed against his will (through the tears of his wife) is not a changed man at all.

I have known women who use their tears to get their way, and it apparently seems to work. But though a husband may bend to the emotional pressure, he may also build resentment which surfaces later in a disastrous way. If he finds someone who is not trying to control him by playing on his emotions, he may even walk out on his marriage. This may seem extreme, but it is a reality all too often. We don't gain respect and we certainly don't promote communication and love by using these emotions as weapons.

Communication Breaker #7: Jesting, joking, and foolish speaking

When Alane and I were visiting a friend shortly after our marriage, he noticed that we often engaged in teasing remarks or making little "fun" jabs at each other. We thought these were quite normal, but our friend begged to differ. Towards the end of our visit, he told us that we had better stop that kind of interaction.

"It's very destructive to a relationship," he counseled.

We took his advice to heart, and for many years now, that manner of speaking has not been a part of our marriage. Instead, we encourage a joyful and happy atmosphere that does not include artificial humor, foolish speaking, or words that demean each other.

Sometimes people who have a difficult time with awkward pauses fill those uncomfortable gaps by trying to be funny or speaking foolishly. Men in particular are prone to this type of speaking. It is hard to imagine Jesus speaking foolishly to his disciples and then saying, "I was just kidding." The counsel of Colossians 4:6 is still relevant today: "Let your speech be always with grace."

For Better or For ~~Worse~~ Best

Even when spoken in fun, cutting remarks made to generate a laugh have a subtle way of undermining relationships and straining communication. Though seemingly innocent comments may seem funny at the time, they have a damaging effect. By putting one spouse down and elevating the other, they may create division. Dishonest remarks lead to distrust and unbelief, so that when true statements are made, they are confused with the exaggerated, flippant responses made in the past. We need to say what we mean and mean what we say—for this is how our words are really interpreted in the heart and mind of our spouse. Your marriage will be much happier if you put energy into building each other up, rather than belittling or tearing each other down just to get a laugh.

We encourage you to prayerfully identify and remove the communication breakers discussed in this chapter, together with any other things that hinder your communication with your spouse. With God's help you, too, can communicate more effectively. As you cooperate with your Heavenly Father, you can become the couple He intended you to be, enjoying a true heart-to-heart marriage that will honor and glorify Him.

Chapter Ten

Respect and Restraint

*I*t was late Sunday afternoon and we were on our way home after a weekend getaway. On the Illinois toll road, we were creeping along in bumper-to-bumper traffic. At the rate things were going, there was no doubt that it would be a long time before we got home.

Suddenly Tom surprised me by cutting across five lanes of traffic and heading for an exit that was quite a bit north of the one we usually took.

"We're going to get lost and waste more time than if we just stayed on this road," I immediately thought. Realizing that my feelings of dismay at the route he was taking were not constructive, I waited a moment before speaking.

"Honey, do you know where you're going?" I asked in the sweetest tone that my doubting heart could muster. Though not wanting to start an argument, I was hoping that if I avoided accusing Tom of not knowing where he was going, he would reconsider his decision. Much to my dismay, and though I was quite unconvinced, he assured me that he knew where he was going.

As the divided highway ended and narrowed down to two lanes, I became increasingly certain that Tom would soon have us lost.

"Honey, are you sure you know where you're going?" I asked again in a sweet, controlled manner. "Maybe we should stop and ask for directions."

Silence reigned as Tom continued to drive. Apparently, we had passed all the gas stations. For him to stop now would mean to imply he was lost, which was simply too much to hope for. Finally, Tom turned to me and asked me to look at the map. I quickly complied, though doubting it would do any good. The road we were traveling was a new one, and likely not on our map. After spending some time matching crossroads and trying to find where we were, my fears were confirmed. We had wasted a lot

For Better or For ~~Worse~~ Best

of time, wherever we were was definitely not on the map, and we would be getting home even later than we had hoped for.

I felt very frustrated about it all, but didn't want to spoil our memories of a nice weekend by letting on my true feelings.

"I can't find our location," I told Tom. He wasn't happy that I couldn't find where we were on the map and he let me know it. I didn't say anything, but I didn't have to. Tension mounted and filled the air as it became obvious that he was determined to continue following his "shortcut." Soon our two-lane paved road became gravel. After a few minutes it was just plain old dirt, which, to Tom's chagrin and humiliation, ended abruptly in a cornfield.

"I told you so!" I felt like saying, though I hadn't told Tom anything. I had only questioned him. While he now had to admit that he was lost and had made a mistake in taking the exit, I sat in cold silence looking out my window. His stubbornness upset me, but I decided not to say a word, leaving him in his "fix." Even though I had tried to mask my displeasure by choosing my words carefully and controlling my tone of voice, in reality I had not been respectful to him. Though I never did say, "I told you so!" my cold, intolerant silence spoke volumes.

Though Tom and I had grown significantly in our marriage by this time, we were still struggling with the principles we now refer to as "respect and restraint." We learned the hard way that a lack of respect and restraint leads to misunderstanding and hurt, even when painful feelings are not expressed. Though we loved each other deeply, when these two pivotal qualities weren't exercised in our thoughts, we were destined to fall into the defensive, self-justifying, "me-focus" mode. Because we didn't understand these concepts, a pleasant weekend together ended in frustration, blame, and a cold war.

Despite whatever directional challenges Tom had, he felt an inherent need (as all men do) to be respected by his wife. A man feels loved when his wife respects his leadership and authority, supporting him both in the home and in public. If we say that we love our husband, but undermine his authority and show no respect for his leadership, he has no reason to believe us.

"Actions speak louder than words" is especially true when it comes to respect. This God-given respect for my husband and restraint of my own

Respect and Restraint

selfish desires was an area where, as God showed me, I needed to improve for the continued success of our marriage.

Webster's Dictionary defines respect as the act of regarding with pleasure, looking favorably upon, or esteeming with real worth. In 1 Corinthians 13, the Bible tells us that respect in love is patient (suffers long), unselfish (seeks not her own), and kind.

With regard to restraint, the dictionary defines it as "to hold back or hinder." Similarly, 1 Corinthians 13 tells us that those who exercise restraint in love are not easily provoked, and do not behave in an unruly manner.

During the lowest period of our marriage, when I was immersed in the "me" focus, I would throw out a specific Bible verse when I wasn't getting my way and all else had failed: "Wives, submit yourselves therefore unto your own husbands" (Ephesians 5:22).

I never quoted the end of the verse—"as unto the Lord"—because that wasn't to my advantage. I also ignored verse 25 of the same chapter, though I was very well aware of it ("Husbands, love your wives even as Christ loved the church and gave Himself for it). What I wanted was leverage for getting my way. Other tactics husbands may use would include yelling at their wives, or going around them, to accomplish the same thing.

These types of inappropriate dominance are not how a man gains the respect of his wife, however. I wouldn't be sharing this illustration if I couldn't also share the rest of the story, which is the best part: there *is* life-changing power in Jesus Christ. I have discovered that if we are willing to whole-heartedly and unconditionally surrender our selfish hearts to Him, to allow Him to give us new hearts and to put a new Spirit within us and cause us to walk in His ways (Ezekiel 36:26, 27), we will learn to love again. Then we will become not only respectful, but respectable men in Christ. We can experience the joy of the power of His Spirit as it restrains our naturally selfish hearts and enables us to experience His new heart in us.

For Better or For ~~Worse~~ Best

As a woman, my natural response was to come out fighting against the verse in Ephesians about respect and submission. "Why should I submit to his unreasonableness?" I thought, and, "What about my rights?" It sounded like a control issue to me. As I grew in grace, however, I realized that while God was not asking me to be a doormat or allow myself to be kicked around, He does want me to surrender my heart to Him. God also wants me, by faith, to choose to allow Tom to be the leader of our home. Only then, as I submit to the leadership of both God and my husband in my life, can my home experience love and harmony in place of strife and contention.

*If we will by faith ask God to give us a heart to love and respect our husbands, He **will** do it. There is nothing too hard for Him (Jeremiah 32:27), including our own heart. As the Holy Spirit restrains us from having our own way, our love and respect for our husbands will grow. Under this restraining influence we will experience real peace and joy in our heart, and happiness and harmony in our marriage.*

Like all married men, I have an inherent need to feel respected by my wife. I also had, and continue to have, high expectations for how Alane would care for my needs. But as a husband, I also had to learn to be sensitive about how I was treating my wife. My desire to be respected by my wife also carries with it a responsibility and privilege that many men often miss or shun. Simply said, men like to feel they are in charge, but are often unwilling to faithfully take up the responsibilities that earn respect and build their wife's trust. And respect is a two-way street.

If I had respected Alane's sense of direction, I might have consulted her before taking the ill-fated "shortcut." But I wanted to do things my way and not be restrained. This happens to many married couples who disagree on a point, yet the human, unrestrained self wants to continue holding to their position. As I thought about our experience, I realized that even though I was not intending selfishness, and my desire was to get us home earlier, my self-sufficiency resisted restraint and pushed aside my respect for Alane. When I recognized this, I took it honestly before God, praying for His grace and power to apply these principles of respect and restraint in our marriage.

Respect and Restraint

When applied in our everyday life, these principles can really impact our decisions. If I had respected Tom according to these definitions, I wouldn't have assumed that we would get lost whenever he took a shortcut. Instead, by placing his decision under the better motive of trying to get us home faster, I would have looked favorably upon him. At the same time, if Tom had truly respected me, he would not have been afraid to ask for my opinion before taking the "shortcut." Together we could have looked at a map, talked openly about our options, and reached an agreement without the loss of time and self-control.

The real power to demonstrate respect comes from being individually surrendered to God, under the influence of His Holy Spirit. Changing our behavior on an outward level, as I tried to do when I carefully answered Tom about the shortcut, doesn't work when the root problem is a heart not at peace. I had allowed agitation to grow, which in turn influenced what I thought and how I responded. God wants to change our hearts, from the inside out.

I am a licensed real-estate broker, although not active in sales anymore. One day I was driving down a very rough and remote road, showing some property to a couple. While the husband and I engaged in a lively conversation, the wife sat quietly between us. At one point she spotted a large rock ahead in the road. I saw it too, but the husband did not.

"Honey, do you see that rock in the road?" she asked in a very respectful way.

"Who's driving?" was his cynical and sarcastic reply. "Don't you think I have eyes?" I was embarrassed for the woman, who was belittled and demeaned by the comment and the tone in which it was delivered. Her countenance fell and she looked as though she wanted to disappear.

What was she to do? If she had remained silent, her husband quite likely would have hit the rock, and then been upset that she hadn't told him there was a rock in the road. Caught between a "rock and a hard

For Better or For ~~Worse~~ Best

place," she just couldn't win! Here was an example of a man who was not respectful to his wife, though she was respectful to him.

During our engagement Tom and I spent a lot of time discussing our wedding and plans for our future. As we were discussing various topics one evening the subject of pets came up. As we talked it soon became apparent that his favorite animal was a dog while mine was a cat. Since we had different preferences and were both working full-time, we decided we would not have any pets until we had children. We also agreed that if we had a girl we would get a cat, and if we had a boy we would get a dog. We ended our discussion in agreement that this was a good solution.

Shortly after our first child was born I reminded Tom of our agreement. Much to my amazement, he had no recollection of the conversation, let alone the agreement. I tried to refresh his memory, but he honestly didn't remember, nor was he interested in having a pet at that time. I respected his decision and didn't think about it again until our second child was born. Again, I reminded him of our conversation, but to no avail.

I could have hounded Tom until he "remembered" the conversation the way I did, or outwardly complied with his decision while inwardly thinking about how selfish, unfair, and unreasonable he was. Or perhaps there would have been other ways to get what I wanted. Because I chose to respect him, however, I took a different path, following the advice of the Bible that wives should not only respect their husbands, but exercise godly restraint through the power of Christ (Ephesians 5:22-24).

As our children grew older, we sometimes came across people in shopping malls who were giving away kittens. Being quite taken with these little balls of fur, my children would inevitably ask if they could have one. While I would have enjoyed having one myself, I respected my husband's wishes and agreed with him that because of our commitments it was not practical to have any pets.

"The kittens are certainly cute," I would tell the children, "but it's just not working out for us to have one right now." I never told the children that I would love to have a kitten and it was their father that didn't want one. If I had undermined my husband's authority in this way, the

Respect and Restraint

children would have learned to play us against each other, losing respect for both of us in the process.

The combination of mutual respect and godly restraint is one of the most powerful aspects in building trust and open communication between a husband and wife. How refreshing it is to feel that your spouse truly respects your thoughts on a subject—so much so that he or she is willing to exercise restraint in order to listen intently and understand what you mean before speaking!

On the other hand, most of us can easily remember how it felt at times when we were shown little or no respect. When we feel a lack of respect, it tempts us to cut corners and conclude that it's not worth even trying to communicate or work through our misunderstandings. As all-too-many couples have found, this response can quickly develop barriers that seriously damage a marriage. In the medical profession, doctors learn to look for the root cause of an illness. Finding the root cause of trouble, which is often a lack of respect and restraint, is also important in a marriage.

Respect and restraint are companions. It's not possible for true respect to govern our thoughts and feelings in the absence of restraint. Respect and restraint are both gifts from God, Who desires to place them in our hearts and marriages so we can experience true love.

In our shortcut illustration, if I had experienced the sweet restraining influence of God's Spirit, I would not have been **trying** *to control my words and manner of speaking. Instead my words and actions would have exhibited, by a genuinely sweet demeanor, the change that had already occurred in my heart through the power of God. If Tom had been willing to experience the restraint of God's Spirit, he would not have pushed past my inquiry when I asked if he knew where he was going.*

No matter how hard we try, we will never experience genuine heart-to-heart love in our marriages without first allowing God to be the Master of our own hearts. We can apply the principles shared in this book, and they will no doubt have a positive affect on our marriage. But,

For Better or For ~~Worse~~ Best

applied only in the weakness of our human effort, we will never gain the changed heart that God longs for in each one of us. If you have never accepted Jesus to be the Lord and Master of your life, choose Him now and invite Him into your heart. Ask Him to guide your life and govern your thoughts and feelings. You have nothing to lose and everything to gain as you experience the positive difference, in your personal life as well as in your marriage.

Following are some simple and practical, yet powerful, principles that couples can implement as they seek to develop respect and restraint in their marriages:

1) Cultivate the spirit of kindness

Ephesians 4:32 says, "Be ye kind one to another, tenderhearted. ..." When actually put into practice in our marriages, this single Bible principle is a powerful tool for building respect and restraint.

As I grew closer to God and surrendered my heart to Him, I learned to implement this principle—even in my driving. At one time, the speed limit in our state was referred to as R & P (for "reasonable and prudent"). Based on weather conditions, it was up to the driver to determine what R & P was.

One day Alane and I were travelling to town at what I considered to be a very reasonable and prudent speed. The sky was blue, the roads were dry, and I was making great time. When Alane asked me if I could slow down, my natural reaction would have been to ask curtly, "Who's driving?" Despite all the things I had learned and experienced, that was still my first inclination. Under the restraining power of the Spirit of God, however, I didn't have to spew out the first thought that came into my mind. In that same moment I heard the prompting of the Holy Spirit speak to my conscience, "Let every man be swift to hear, slow to speak, slow to wrath" (James 1:19). Quickly I made the choice to reject the first thought, listen to the heart of my wife, and ask the Holy Spirit to guide me to a better response.

His Spirit prompted me to tell my wife that when she was in the car with me, I would drive a speed that made the ride enjoyable for

Respect and Restraint

her, and when I was alone I would drive a speed the Lord and I agreed was reasonable. There was no audible voice, and maybe not those exact words, only the simple promptings that come to any person willing to yield self to know the will of God. Slowing down was a simple way for me to cultivate kindness toward Alane, and her request provided a beautiful opportunity for me to experience God's gentle restraint by respecting her reasonable wishes and comfort. Here lies the essence of how the power of the gospel works together with our choices.

It really touched me when Tom agreed to slow down and explained why he would. I knew he had not arrived at this choice on his own, but that God had impressed him with these thoughts. It meant so much to me that he cared more about my comfort and God's will than he did about getting to town a few minutes earlier. I also felt relieved that, even in my absence, Tom would drive under the Lord's guidance. This gave me additional peace about his safety.

It is my desire to be kind to Tom and thoughtful of his wishes. Sometimes, however, I've caught myself wanting to do something special for him—something that communicates a message of love—yet carrying it out in a way that doesn't demonstrate kindness.

One day I asked Tom what he wanted for our afternoon meal, then suggested something easy to make before he had a chance to respond. The Holy Spirit reminded me that I had asked Tom a question but not given him a chance to answer. Instead of preparing the easy meal I had suggested, I decided to make homemade pizza, a gourmet salad, steamed vegetables, and a dessert. Then I set the table with a nice tablecloth, candles, and silk flowers and put on some soft music before letting Tom know that dinner was ready. I'm sure you can imagine his surprise when he arrived at the table expecting something much more simple. It was thrilling to have him sit down to a special meal that I had prepared just for him.

There are hundreds of ways that we can cultivate kindness in our marriages. Kindness doesn't require money, a special environment, or exceptional skills; it only requires a willingness to let God influence our hearts and minds. Make the decision to practice this principle today.

For Better or For ~~Worse~~ Best

*Prayerfully consider what God wants you to do to **cultivate the spirit of kindness** toward your spouse before the day closes.*

2) Determine never to injure your spouse

Though simple, this second principle also helps develop respect and restraint. We don't have to understand "deep things" in order to allow God to transform our marriages. If we apply practical principles such as being **"determined never to injure the other person"** within our marriages, God can work mightily in our lives.

We might think that being determined not to injure our spouse by our words, actions, reactions, or passions would come spontaneously and naturally. After all, we love each other! If we are not careful, however, we can easily injure one another through these. It is usually when we least expect it that something happens to initiate a selfish response that may hurt the one we love. Human love is not enough. We need God's divine love working in our hearts to make the difference.

One time, a couple requested a counseling session outside of our normal ministry hours. Because of the many demands on our time, we had committed to special family time each evening. This carefully guarded time not only demonstrated to our children that they were a priority but also reinforced our commitment to "practice what we preached."

This couple was aware we didn't take evening ministry calls, but because their need was urgent, we prayerfully made an exception. Before the appointment Alane and I discussed the principles involved in their situation and how we should handle the call. We also agreed we would keep the conversation short, focused on the issue at hand, and return to our family commitment as soon as was appropriate. The call came as expected; we prayed together, sympathized with their situation, and discussed the principles involved for the desired solution.

As the conversation began to wind down it became apparent that Alane was not finished. Remembering our commitment to family time, I decided to gracefully bow out of the conversation and make my way upstairs where Alane was on the phone, gain eye contact, and give her

Respect and Restraint

a signal it was time to end the conversation. As I started up the stairs, the Lord called to my conscience in that "still, small voice." I became aware that my perspective and desire for her to wrap up the call were not God's way. I realized this approach was not respectful and could hurt my wife. The Lord impressed me with His approach, which was to make eye contact with Alane and simply give her a genuine, heartfelt smile that would communicate her freedom to continue. When I recognized how much better God's approach was than mine, I made it my own. By the time I got to the top of the stairs I had fully surrendered and was empowered by God to carry out His plan.

When I heard Tom coming up the stairs, I thought he would give me a signal to end the conversation. Instead, he gave me a sincere smile from his heart. I was pleased to see that, even though I had failed to keep the conversation as short as we had hoped, the Lord was working in Tom's heart. These little examples of God's redeeming grace in our hearts motivate both of us to continue to make choices by faith in what God can do, rather than being driven by selfish feelings of the moment. In return, God brings a joy and a deepening love to our marriage that is beyond our imagination.

Let God put respect and restraint into your marriage. Cultivate kindness and be determined never to injure the one by your side. You can build a better marriage than you've ever had before.

Chapter Eleven

Setting Goals and Priorities

When I was a young girl I dreamed of being a missionary nurse. I can still remember the stories I heard and read about nurses in foreign lands, helping to save lives and bringing people to the knowledge of Jesus as their personal Savior. Throughout my school years my parents were supportive of my dreams and goals and did whatever they could to help me achieve them. I learned to be self-motivated, to study diligently, and to do my best. Six months after I graduated from high school, I was accepted into a two-year nursing school program. In addition to keeping my GPA high for scholarship purposes, I had to work to help pay my way through. Because of how things worked out, I also took an overload of classes. It was very challenging to say the least, but my dream was in the making and my goal was becoming closer to reality. After finishing the nursing program in one and a half years and having written my Nursing Board Exams to receive my RN, I left for the mission field. I was so excited! I was going to Nicaragua. Finally, I would be a real missionary nurse!

My mission experience turned out to be one of the greatest blessings of my life. It was more than I had dreamed of; fulfilling, yet often challenging. I was part of a team of four nurses who were responsible for all the health care in a jungle region. We had to diagnose and treat illnesses, deliver babies in bamboo huts crawling with cockroaches, and handle all types of trauma. In addition to our work and household duties, we reached out with the love of Jesus to the villagers, befriending them, visiting in their homes, and providing weekly services for them and their children.

Looking back on it now, I realize because I had a dream to be a nurse, I planned for that goal, worked for it, and made it a priority. I

For Better or For ~~Worse~~ Best

thought nothing of the long hours of school and difficult tests. I was willing to work hard to reach my goal.

As Tom and I counsel couples who have marital problems, I sometimes wonder how many of them have goals for their marriage.

"Has it really been the goal of each person to find the love of their life, get married, and live happily ever after?" I ask myself.

Though these are worthy goals, most couples are falling far short of achieving them. When they hit bumps on the road, some have detoured while others have crashed. A big reason for these failures, I believe, is that the goals most couples have are too broad and generic. In addition, not enough time or attention has been spent deciding how to practically meet those goals. The key is to take those goals and priorities out of the closet, discuss them openly, and put a plan in place in our daily lives in order to realize their fulfillment.

How ironic it is that, while we understand the importance of goals and priorities in achieving success in the workplace or for our children's education, we often miss the importance of goals for our marriages.

An executive illustrated this point very well to me once. He could manage people well, and millions of corporate dollars, but he floundered in the management of his own family and their finances, and this was very frustrating to him. The primary reason for his success at work was the clear set of corporate objectives that he was expected to meet. As we talked he also saw that he was not doing this same kind of goal setting, followed by priority planning, on the home front. It wasn't because he was incapable or unwilling. He was just so busy at work that he hadn't recognized the necessity of applying those same goal-setting and organizational principles in his home life.

Once he made this practical connection and started making his marriage and family the priority it should have been, things began to change for the better. As his priorities began to shift to accommodate the needs of his family, he put energy into goal-setting and relationship-building. As a result, his wife and children received a real blessing in his leadership under Christ!

Setting Goals and Priorities

We need to set goals in life, or life will just continue on without direction, purpose or even fulfillment. We need to take the time to evaluate our lives and determine if the direction we are going is actually leading us to our goal. We need to determine what goals are important to us and how we are going to go about reaching them. If we don't, we will find ourselves simply existing instead of growing and thriving.

Most of us discussed goals and priorities before we were married, but we must continue to keep them before us and routinely evaluate our progress. The benefit we have found as we consistently communicate in these matters is that it always leads to greater unity, purpose, and direction.

If you have never set goals for your lives, there is no better time than now to begin. First, discuss your goals and begin to set priorities that will help you to achieve those goals. You will find that in so doing you will naturally be drawn closer together, that you will love and respect each other more, and that you will be working together instead of against each other.

To illustrate this process, we would like to share some of the goals that were important to us then and continue to be important to us now, and how we learned to set our priorities in order to make them a reality.

The Goals of Our Married Life

Goal #1: A happy home

Happy homes do not happen spontaneously! Most of what happens spontaneously ends up being the negative things in life—like weeds in the garden. The plants that we want in our garden take planning, planting, and cultivating to reap the desired results. In order to have a happy home we must set priorities to ensure success.

Psalm 133:1 tells us "how good and pleasant it is ... to dwell together in unity." If we first have unity personally with Christ, we will then be prepared to have unity in our marriages, which will in turn set the foundation for a happy home. This goal continues to be so important to us that we prioritize our lives to keep our home happy.

For Better or For ~~Worse~~ Best

When problems arise, we work from cause to effect to determine why things are not going well. We have found that when we're truly willing to be honest about the cause (usually falling into the "me" focus), we can always find a solution. Once it is identified, we make a personal choice to deal with the solution in Christ. Pain and unhappiness only continue if one or both of us recognize the problem but refuse to cooperate with heaven's power to overcome.

Our home is very happy for one simple reason: choosing to follow God's way with the help of God's power transforms our hearts, bringing true peace and happiness. You can have this same happiness and a marriage that is heart to heart if you are willing to submit your will to God's will for your life. As you truly surrender yourself to Christ you will receive the answers you seek and experience the power you need to follow His way.

Goal #2: Gaining and maintaining a vital connection with Christ

Early on in our marriage, we both understood the importance of taking time for prayer, study of the word, and communion with God, yet quite honestly, we weren't giving Him very much time. The press and push of life made prayer time a short and mind-wandering experience. We didn't take time to "be still and know that I am God" (Psalm 46:10).

In order for us to experience the reality of becoming living, practicing Christians, this time of vital connection with Him had to take first place in our lives. The goal, to become like Christ and have our characters changed into His likeness, could only happen as we made time daily to first gain and then to maintain a real connection to the power of Christ.

It isn't so much our level of knowledge, but rather how the knowledge we do have affects how we live. In 1 John 5:12 we are told, "He that hath the Son hath life and he that hath not the Son of God hath not life." Do you have His life working in you, guiding you, keeping you and empowering you to live above your selfishness? If not, why not make the goal of being a living Christian the most important one in your life, and begin to make this happen by making your time with God the first priority of every day?

Setting Goals and Priorities

Goal #3: To have a family

We both loved children, and decided before we were married that we would have children after we had our own home. We both worked during our first year of marriage, making it a priority to save enough money for a down payment. About nine months into our marriage we began to look for our first home. After some searching, we found an ideal home just a mile and a half from our workplace. We made an offer, and were delighted when it was accepted! Much to our surprise, just days after all the transactions were completed we found out that our first child was on her way.

Though we had planned to have children, we hadn't meant to be parents this early in our marriage. Now we had to set new priorities in order to be ready for this event. Since we had already agreed that I would be a full-time mommy when we had children, we re-evaluated our expenditures and adjusted our course in order to tighten up our finances so we could live on one income. I am thankful to say that by this time we had a solid marriage and had learned to work through challenges. Holding to our commitment to be full-time parents for our children, we set our course united. We have learned from experience that as we are willing to work together with each other and with God, He makes the impossible become a possibility.

Eight months later our daughter was born. In order to maintain my nursing skills and meet our financial commitments (which had been based on two full-time incomes), I did work one day each week. Because of our commitment to our goals, however, we never gave in to pressure or temptation for me to go back to work in order to meet financial demands. We learned to live simply and be content with less.

Goal #4: Parenting in agreement

This was a goal we set as we considered the importance of unity in our marriage for our own happiness as well as the future happiness of our children.

For Better or For ~~Worse~~ Best

In Romans 15:5 we are admonished to allow "the God of patience and consolation (to) grant you to be like-minded one toward another according to Christ Jesus." In practical terms, this means to harmonize our way of thinking with the mind of Christ. If we disagree on parenting issues, we need to willingly and openly seek the principles of God's Word. If we are willing, He will bring our minds into like-mindedness with Him, and His way is always better than our way.

Early on, Alane and I "agreed not to disagree" in front of our children. If we didn't agree, we would wait for a time when we could discuss our thoughts in private and seek God's will together. We have sometimes failed in this last point, but have certainly seen the blessing of success in following this principle the majority of the time.

Goal #5: Lifestyle and daily schedule

It was after Tom and I had two children that we came face to face with the importance of lifestyle and a daily schedule in a very dramatic way. It was a rare, quiet Friday evening. We had been enjoying some family time when out of the blue Tom asked me, "What is the most important thing you can accomplish in your life?" I reflected on the last hour of our evening. Everything seemed just perfect; the girls were happy, Tom and I had a good conversation, and we were enjoying that feeling of family togetherness. Then my thoughts turned to the future and I answered, "To see our children in heaven, and see the crown of life placed on their heads." There was silence, and then Tom said, "Then something has got to change and that something is us!"

That night I gathered my family around me and prayed a prayer of consecration and commitment to the Lord. I said, "Lord, I'm willing to give up anything, I'll go wherever You want me to go, I'll do anything You ask me to do, in order to hear the words, 'Well done, thou good and faithful servant' and to see our children receive the crown of life." From that night, the way we viewed life, our goals, and how we set priorities began to change. It was not that we suddenly became

Setting Goals and Priorities

enlightened with new ideas, but rather that we made a commitment to prioritize what we already knew.

As we faced the reality of our daily lives, we both intuitively knew that the way we were living was not preparing our girls, or even ourselves, for heaven. We were too caught up in the temporal life, with very little thought of eternity. At the time, we were not having regular family worship. We were not really training our girls to be like Jesus—obedient, kind, patient, etc. We were letting their little "selves" rule when they were crossed. This was displayed in various ways, none of which was Christ-like.

Once we came face to face with our own lack, we began immediately to adjust our course and make necessary changes. First we implemented a daily schedule that included a set time to get up and set time to go to bed. We also established regular meal times and nap times for the girls, as well as morning and evening worship times. This brought a spiritual focus to our lives on a daily basis. We began to see the need to train our children in the right way that would develop their characters for heaven. The verse, "Train up a child in the way he should go, and when he is old he will not depart from it" (Proverbs 22:6), became our focus throughout the day. Rather than allowing our children to drift through each day in their own mode of play and self-gratification, we began teaching and training them. As we began to make these needed changes, we experienced positive results in our entire family. Our girls were more content and happy. I was more orderly, efficient, and patient. Tom was committed to personal time with God and clear in the direction he was to lead our family.

All of these things led to a happier environment, a more peaceful life, and a greater awareness of the reality of heaven in our home. It was not long after this that the Lord led us from our suburban home to the mountains of Montana. There we were able to raise our children in the country, which had been one of our goals since before we were married.

For Better or For ~~Worse~~ Best

In building not just a better marriage, but the best marriage possible, we want to encourage you to take time to talk about what is important to each of you and to formulate goals. Look for ways to blend these goals, making them "us" focused, and then begin immediately to set priorities to meet these goals. As you take the time to set these goals and priorities, realizing that they can only be achieved through Christ, you will soon begin to experience the blessings that God has in store for you.

Chapter Twelve

Moral Purity for Men

The day I married Alane, I made a commitment to her and to God. Even in my ignorance, I understood that my eyes were to be for my wife only—that looking at other women with lustful thoughts would not only be unacceptable, but destructive to our marriage.

As a man, there are important avenues I must guard in order to maintain moral purity. What I choose to look at, read, and even what I listen to can affect me in this regard. Philippians 4:8 is a very helpful scripture in evaluating whether or not what we choose to put into our minds will maintain moral purity: "Whatsoever things are true, whatsoever things are honest ... just ... pure ... lovely ... of a good report, if there be any virtue, and if there be any praise, think on these things."

The fact that men are easily stimulated by what they see makes it all the more important to make a conscious commitment about it. This commitment, which addresses how you will deal with the things you see and what you will think about in relation to women, must be made to God and your wife.

Though Job was a righteous, God-fearing man, he understood the avenue of the eyes for the fleshly, carnal nature. In Job 31:1, he describes his covenant with God: "I made a covenant with mine eyes; why then should I look upon a maid?" This doesn't mean that Job never "saw" a women who passed by while he sat in the gate. Rather, Job was simply describing his commitment to be consciously aware of the direction his thoughts were headed. If those thoughts were going in the wrong direction, Job had a commitment to shun or dismiss them. His commitment was to have "clean hands and a pure heart" (Psalm 24:4). Only

For Better or For ~~Worse~~ Best

those with "clean hands" (righteous works) and a "pure heart" (right thoughts, moral purity) will live with God eternally. It's not wrong to look at a woman. It's what you do with the look—and why you continue to look—that can be destructive. Over the years, I have counseled many men who were struggling with fantasizing, wandering eyes, and/or pornography. Each of these practices is connected with masturbation or unnatural, brutish, sexual aggression toward their wife. Such habits are absolutely lethal to the achievement of mutually meaningful intimacy. If you are trapped in one of these snares, I entreat you—for your sake and that of your wife—to make a covenant with your eyes to God. Enter into this commitment with your wife and enlist her support and encouragement to be faithful. Pray daily for God to give you "clean hands and a pure heart," then be mindful not to place yourself in the way of temptation.

"Flee also youthful lusts: but follow righteousness, faith, charity, peace, with them that call on the Lord out of a pure heart" (2 Timothy 2:22). This scripture is a powerful safeguard. Whether applied to the TV, Internet, newspaper, radio, iPods, books, or the content of conversations, it can strengthen the moral sensibilities.

Is that TV sitcom you are watching passing the test? If not, don't watch it—it will undermine your moral purity. Is that pop-up on the Internet that arouses your curiosity going to lead you in a wrong direction? Prayerfully resist the temptation to pursue that curiosity. Is that book you are reading true or a novel? Is it edifying your marriage or causing you to fantasize or be discontent or disconnected from your spouse? Give yourself wholly to God and ask Him to remove these destructive influences from your life.

Almost all forms of media share a set of similar and all-too-familiar themes: sex, immorality, lust, passion, violence, aggression, and suspense. What we see and hear does become a part of us, transforming who we are. Though gradual and imperceptible at first, the impact is real. There is a simple yet powerful and unchangeable law: by beholding we become changed! One of the reasons many are unhappy in their marriages is because Hollywood portrays that love is based on appearance and sex. The same is true for romance novels that captivate so many today. The music of the day, with its driving rhythms and

Moral Purity for Men

lyrics, also imbed a message of immoral conduct. Meanwhile, pop-up messages on the Internet entice our passions. It is up to us to decide in advance to say "NO" to these craftily calculated intrusions.

It is time that we take the moral purity of our hearts and marriages seriously. Through the mighty power of a living Savior, we can put an end to these influences in our lives and homes. The key is for us to realize that, by ourselves, we are no match for the lusts of our flesh or the pride of life. But we can be encouraged by Jesus' words, "But be of good cheer; I have overcome the world" (John 16:33).

Modesty in dress is another area that men really need to look out for. This is not just a women's issue! Extremely tight clothing is not modest. Some men's swimsuits are so skimpy and tight that they are grossly immodest. Men as well as women should be careful about how they dress, taking care not to draw undue attention to themselves.

Modesty in deportment is also important for men. It is possible to dress modestly, yet carry oneself in a way that conveys moral impurity to others. The ideas we cherish, the thoughts that we think, will all be communicated in the aura about us, and sooner or later will work their way into our words and actions.

Foolish jesting, telling off-color jokes, or even laughing at them brings up serious questions that must be addressed by those seeking to experience mutually meaningful intimacy. In today's world, men have become more comfortable in making suggestive sexual comments. The result is an open door for moral impurity in both men and women.

The lack of reserve in a man is what often places him in the position of being too familiar with a woman. Undo familiarity can unconsciously remove God-given barriers and can lead to an improper relationship very quickly, even if there is nothing physical involved. This is not just a woman's matter. Men should take the lead, by conducting themselves in a reserved and thoughtful manner when interacting with other women. Flirtatious comments, light bantering, witticisms, and even joking are not acceptable, as they tend to break down the natural reserve.

It is totally inappropriate for a man to find a confidential friend in a female. This does not mean we cannot be cordial or have women as friends. It does mean, however, that we don't enter into communication that should only be shared with our wives. Placing confidence in a female co-worker or friend will undermine the intimacy of communication with your wife.

As a husband, I am praying and looking for ways to meet the needs of my wife. I pray for God to equip me daily to be the "houseband," the husband upon whom my wife can depend for leadership, for encouragement, for tender compassion, and to meet the harsh demands of this world. These thoughts may be considered "old-fashioned" in some circles, but I assure you, they are critical to safeguarding your marriage. Moral purity is also inseparably linked to meaningful intimacy. The good news is that, as we make it a serious matter of prayer and commitment, our marriages will be strengthened and safeguarded against the impurities all around us.

Chapter Thirteen

Moral Purity for Women

*W*omen have just as much responsibility in maintaining moral purity in marriage as do men. While men may be more visually stimulated, women are drawn in through their emotions. This is why it is so important to keep our thoughts channeled in a positive way toward our husband. If we are feeling hurt or misunderstood or if communication is lacking, we are more prone to be flattered by the attentions of another man.

I have seen these principles in action on several occasions. One young couple who I worked with at the hospital became caught up in the busyness of life. In time—because they were so busy—communication lessened. Their marriage just wasn't as vibrant as it had been before.

She was a very talented secretary and in time took a career advancement as an executive secretary. Her new boss, who was very impressed with her ability and efficiency, paid her many compliments at work. These compliments reached her heart, which began to open to him. Soon his comments grew into flattering statements not only about her work, but her personal beauty as well. Instead of recognizing the danger of such words, she soaked them in like a sponge. Her boss, who could see her receptiveness, soon took another step forward in breaking down her guard. First it was a hand on her shoulder while standing at her desk, then a grasp of her hand when she handed him some papers. With every advance she responded until, in time, more physical attention was shown— a hug, a kiss, and finally an affair that painfully affected both marriages.

Though neither she nor her boss intended to have an affair, they failed to govern their thoughts. As a result, they ended up being unfaithful to their spouses. If she would have kept her heart toward her husband, she would have rejected the flattery and kept her heart's door closed to

For Better or For ~~Worse~~ Best

her boss. Like many women, however, she allowed her emotions to take control. As a result, she found herself in a heartbreaking situation.

Thoughts lead to feelings and emotions, which in time express themselves in words and actions. No doubt the wise man understood this when he counseled us to "keep your heart with all diligence, for out of it are the issues of life" *(Proverbs 4:23).*

This is a specific call to our hearts as wives to not let our thoughts take us down "daydream lane" or fanaticize about "what would it be like." As wives, we have a responsibility to keep our thoughts, heart, and emotions affectionately connected to our husbands. If tempted to think about another man, put such thoughts away quickly and focus your mind on all the wonderful things that first drew you to your spouse. Concentrating on what you appreciate about him will turn you from the road of danger by helping you to fall in love with him all over again. If thinking positive thoughts about your husband is a struggle, pray for God's help to think on the good and lovely. He loves to answer such prayers!

Being attentive to how we dress and carry ourselves also plays an important role in maintaining moral purity in our marriage. Here is where many women become defensive.

"No one is going to tell me what to wear!" I have heard so many say. They don't realize that the issue is more than about what we wear—it's about keeping moral purity in our marriage. It is a rule of life that certain attire draws the wrong type of attention, opening the way for inappropriate flattery and/or physical advancement. Whether we realize it or not, our deportment is affected by what we think and how we dress. If we dress in a sexy way, we will also carry ourselves in that manner. On the other hand, if we dress modestly, we will conduct ourselves with proper reserve. The importance of dress upon our actions is another good reason why we should avoid skin-tight clothes that reveal every curve, crack, or bump; low, plunging tops that advertise the bosom to others; and short skirts (even if they are the fashion of the day).

Though men can't read our thoughts, they are very good at reading our aura. A crack in the foundation of a building will have a damaging effect. Similarly, a crack in our moral purity will break down the foundation of our marriage, damaging it over time as well.

Moral Purity for Women

Tell you husband that you are committed to him and to making your marriage vibrantly intimate and morally pure within and without. Let him know that you want to explore with him how to grow in both areas. Ask him if there is anything that you wear that makes him feel embarrassed or uncomfortable when you are in public. Don't be afraid of his response or be defensive.

As wives, we need to be willing to evaluate our hearts in the area of moral purity, asking God to help us change anything that would be keeping us from experiencing the beauty and fulfillment of our marriage vows.

And lastly, let us pray the prayer of King David: "Create in me a clean heart, O God; and renew a right spirit within me" *(Psalm 51:10).*

Chapter Fourteen

Mutually Meaningful Intimacy

Among the many couples we've counseled, some had not engaged in any sexual intimacy for literally months on end. Such couples use the aspect of intimacy to control or punish each other. The reasons were often petty, yet they had been left unresolved. Wives are the ones most likely to withhold themselves in a marriage. If her feelings have been hurt, she may deny her husband to show her displeasure. Men have their own way of reacting, however. Quite often an unhappy husband gratifies his sexual drive as purely a physical act, without the expression of love, tenderness or care. These approaches, while intended to "send a message" or "even the score," only intensify the problems that do exist. While a sexual expression of love is not the cure for problems, neither should it be used as a weapon against the other.

In 1 Corinthians 7:5, NKJV, we are cautioned against withholding marital intimacy. "Do not deprive one another except with consent for a time, that you may give yourselves to fasting and prayer; and come together again so that Satan does not tempt you because of your lack of self-control." Although abstinence may be agreed upon with a specific purpose and for a designated period of time, it should not be born out of resentment, anger, hurt, or imbalance.

In a marriage where both are selfishly taking, only the most stinted and shriveled intimacy can exist. In contrast, the most beautiful, rich, and fulfilling intimacy thrives in a relationship where both give to enrich the other. Jesus said it simply in Luke 6:38: "Give and it shall be given unto you; good measure, pressed down, and shaken together, and running over. …"

For Better or For ~~Worse~~ Best

If only this principle was better understood in the marriage relationship! Mutually meaningful intimacy is not an isolated event, or a selfish, lustful encounter where one or both partners are in the giving or taking mode. So much more than a sexual experience, it incorporates being one in heart and purpose; respecting our spouse and restraining our own selfish nature; learning how to ask for true forgiveness without excusing or justifying ourselves; and learning how to forgive our spouse and forget the wrong done. It includes effective communication as well as developing a harmonious spiritual walk. All of these factors make up a meaningful intimacy that is equally fulfilling to both husband and wife. Intimacy, the beautiful, culminating experience of two people who are fascinated with and dedicated to each other, is the ultimate expression of simultaneous giving and receiving to achieve the blessing of "us." This is the true experience and meaning of "the two shall become one flesh."

If we will learn how to serve our spouse as Jesus served us, we would find our love for them growing. It is when we are selfish and wanting to be served that we find dissatisfaction and unhappiness. As Tom and I have been willing to take the challenge of the biblical principle "in honor, preferring one another" (Romans 12:10), we have experienced the benefits both individually and in our marriage, especially in the area of intimacy. This principle means that I am not seeking for Tom to dote over me, do everything I want, and see everything my way; but rather as I respect his ideas and opinions, support his leadership, and care for his needs, I become a better wife. Tom in turn demonstrates his appreciation and affection toward me in ways that are meaningful to me, rather than what is convenient for him. He expresses his gratitude for my commitment to our family and the way I manage our home. He also respects my opinion.

Many of the keys to building a loving and mutually meaningful intimacy are found in the earlier chapters of this book. Discarding the selfish "me focus" and choosing the "us focus" is crucial to closeness in marriage. This attitude considers what is best for "us" and our marriage—not just what "I want." In addition, take a few minutes to discover the love

Mutually Meaningful Intimacy

language of your spouse and you. This will help you better respond to each others' love language. There is a simple 30-question multiple-choice online test that has proved a blessing to many marriages.

Only in giving do we receive more to give. Only as we unselfishly seek to understand the one by our side do we in turn receive their understanding. And it is only by reaching out with a love that is willing to risk being vulnerable that we receive the love we need.

The privilege and special intimacy that is such a beautiful part of our marriage is really a culmination of trust, of reaching out to one another, and connecting heart to heart. Intimacy isn't just something that occurs because Alane is my wife and therefore should "meet my needs." In Ephesians 4:2 we are told that we should care for each other "with all lowliness and meekness, with longsuffering, forbearing one another in love." Following this principle in our daily interactions stimulates love and trust in each another.

Unfortunately, many issues get in the way of such trust in a marriage. Career demands, "keeping up with the Joneses," the pressures of child-rearing or caring for aging parents, and financial stress are just a few of the factors that often combine to create separation between a husband and wife.

Whether this separation is physical, emotional, or both—it goes against the biblical principle that "two should be one," breaking down mutual trust and meaningful intimacy. All too often, love and tender understanding are replaced by sexually driven lust which is devoid of the special meeting of heart, mind, emotion, and understanding. Without the emotional connection, the sexual experience soon loses its deeper motivation of love and isn't satisfying. The result is a "fatal cycle," not necessarily for the marriage itself, but for the needed mutually meaningful intimacy. The wife begins to feel she is important for only one function. The man realizes that something has changed, but isn't sure what the problem is. In the absence of the deep, heart-to-heart communication, things will inevitably deteriorate. If this condition continues unaddressed, it can lead to such sentiments as:

For Better or For ~~Worse~~ Best

- "I don't have any more feelings."
- "There's no romance left in our relationship."
- "Our sexual experience has lost its meaning."
- "There's no love left."

As Tom and I have implemented God's principles, we have developed a meaningful intimacy that is fulfilling to both of us. Because of his tender regard and love for me, I do not feel like an object, but rather the love of his life. He senses my love and respect, which makes him complete as a man. After more than 30 years of marriage our love for each other, and the deep, meaningful intimacy we experience, just keeps getting richer and more fulfilling.

The degradation in our society has led many people to think of intimacy as only a sexual act, but this doesn't have to be the case in your marriage. If you and your spouse find you have slipped into this state, do not give up on each other or your marriage. Your marriage vows, which constitute a covenant made before others and God, were not dependent on feelings. You made a commitment for better or worse, for richer or poorer, in sickness and health, until death should part you. With God's help, your intimacy can be rebuilt. The process that degrades the beauty of marriage can be reversed. By following God's principles, you can recover all you have lost, and it won't be long before your marriage is fully restored. Don't be discouraged, and do not give up! Get up and go forward in the strength of Jesus Christ!

No doubt you have made many commitments in your life. Perhaps you committed yourself to succeed in college, or in your career, or in other relationships. If you have not done so already, now is the time to give your marriage commitment its rightful place in your life. Determine to take time for communication, and to spend quality time with each other. Prayerfully evaluate where you have been losing ground, then make principled choices to reestablish those "waste places" in your hearts and home.

Chapter Fifteen

Finding Forgiveness

There were times in our marriage when, after a disagreement or outright argument, I would be the first to apologize and ask forgiveness. I always hoped that Alane would also acknowledge her wrong and say she was sorry, and usually there was mutual recognition of wrong and forgiveness. On some occasions, however, she would apologize for something that didn't seem like the *real* issue to me.

"Well, that's not what I want you to be sorry for!" I would sometimes say. Whether intentional or not, this type of response implied that I would only forgive Alane if she came to me on my terms. There is a tendency in all of us, stemming from our selfish nature, to feel like we don't need to forgive unless it is requested. In addition, we somehow like to measure whether the sorrow for sin is sufficient to merit forgiveness.

The forgiving spirit manifested by Christ, which is illustrated by the words, "Father forgive them for they know not what they do" (Luke 23:34), has more to do with the spirit and heart condition of the "forgiver" than with the person asking to be forgiven. This type of forgiveness comes from a **state of mind**, a true willingness on the part of the forgiver that doesn't depend on any other circumstances.

Christ offered an example of this type of forgiveness when he washed His betrayer's feet. In this humble act Judas recognized the heart cry of Jesus to his soul—"How can I give thee up?" Yet he chose to reject Christ and His forgiveness, and will be eternally lost as a result.

Jesus showed us by His example that the forgiveness that breaks down barriers doesn't wait for a request for forgiveness. The forgiveness that comes from above is not dependent upon anything except our willingness to receive it as a gift from God. If we follow the example of

For Better or For ~~Worse~~ Best

Jesus, then we will extend forgiveness to our spouse even if they don't yet know that they need it.

The beauty of this deep, forgiving spirit is how it affects us. There is real freedom in not having our stomach in knots, or in not feeling stressed while waiting for our spouse to apologize for some wrong they may have committed. This peace of mind can happen only as we offer forgiveness, for only then are we free to love. While this may sound unreasonable or even extreme, it is in fact the very love and forgiveness that Jesus modeled for us during His whole life on earth. "While we were yet sinners, (before we were even repentant) Christ died for us" (Romans 5:8).

There is a deep and powerful connection between this kind of forgiveness and true repentance. The more willing we are for God to show us our true sinfulness, and the more willing we are to be honest in our confession and repentance, the more willing we are to be forgiving. Being vulnerable and willing to see the selfishness of our lives apart from Christ also frees us to be honest and specific in our confession of sin to each another. This process also leaves us more desirous to receive that Godly sorrow that will turn us from sin.

It is possible to extend true forgiveness; while not continuing as an enabler of the sin you are forgiving over and over again. Jesus said, "If he trespass against thee seven times in a day, and seven times in a day turn again unto thee, saying, I repent; then thou shalt forgive him" (Luke 17:4). We know that this verse struck deep into the disciples' hearts, for in the next verse Luke tells us that "the apostles [not just Peter] said unto the Lord, Increase our faith." They realized, as we should, that exercising that level of forgiveness could only result when a great deal of faith was involved.

An example would be the story of a man who called me one day, very troubled and upset. He was frustrated that his wife wouldn't leave the past behind; that she was holding him in an "old mold" and not letting him out of the box. While I was quietly praying for wisdom, the thought came to me to ask him if the issues were only in his past or if he was living his past in the present. There was an awkward pause. Then he began to pour out the real story about physically abusing his wife and children, and how his wife told him he must move out. He

Finding Forgiveness

was obviously hurting and fearful and didn't know how to proceed. I asked him if he would consent to have his wife join our conversation. He agreed and called her to the phone. What came out as they shared together was a story of a couple who really loved each other and their children. The wife had forgiven the same offense repeatedly while continuing to love her weak and discouraged husband, but she could no longer allow this behavior to continue. Though she sincerely loved him, and genuinely had God's forgiveness in her heart toward him, she was firmly drawing the line that he could not stay.

At that point, we talked about what I call a "separation for restoration." This means that the couple has bona fide grounds to separate, and both agree they need the separation to help restore their marriage. As I continued to counsel with this couple throughout their separation, I once again saw the living, life-changing power of Christ as their lives were brought back together. The husband told me that what his wife had done was just what he needed. When she drew a firm boundary on his abuse, he was forced to face it for what it really was. But what really broke his heart was experiencing his wife's genuine forgiveness and love toward him. She was able to find the balance in Christ of loving the sinner while hating the sin; demonstrating God's forgiveness without condoning or enabling the sin. This is a divine combination.

I saw this family not long after their marriage was restored. As I observed this couple interacting together and with their children, my heart rejoiced for the miracle-working power of Christ. You'd never know their marriage was nearly broken.

One area that needs to be addressed, as we consider forgiveness, is the "forgetting" that should go along with forgiving. Talking about our spouse's defects and weaknesses with others is one of the deadliest things we can do to destroy our marriage. I am thankful I grew up in a home were the rule was, "If you can't say anything nice, don't say anything at all." My parents practiced what they preached and, following their example, I was usually mindful not to speak negatively about other people.

After I was married, however, I let this standard slip for a time. I became friends with a lady who was married but not very fulfilled, since

For Better or For ~~Worse~~ Best

she had a dictatorial husband. From time to time she would share with me about her trials and unhappiness. Then she would ask me what weaknesses I had found in my husband. Over time, our communication always seemed to go down this path.

I indiscreetly shared with her what I viewed as Tom's faults. Though my complaints were miniscule, she seemed to enjoy hearing them "grow." Interestingly, I began to notice I would become more critical of Tom after spending time with her. Tom also noticed the difference in how I related to him after I'd been with her. Then one morning as I was studying, I read these words: "Let the wife's heart be the grave for her husband's faults."

That one-liner pierced my heart! Conversations I'd had with this woman flashed through my mind, along with the wicked results that followed in my own thoughts and the negative impact on my marriage. I asked God to forgive me and to help me never say another word about my husband's weaknesses to anyone. Furthermore, I asked Him not to let my mind "go there" either. What a powerful transformation God made in my heart! Truly a God of healing, He wants us to experience modern-day miracles like those He performed in days of old.

Not long after my change of heart, I again spent time with this friend. As always, she asked her standard question: "So, how are things with you and Tom?"

"Great!" I was happy to honestly respond. She seemed surprised, and was obviously not convinced.

"How are things really?" she asked again.

"Great!" I responded a second time. She tried one more time to evoke a negative response but I told her I was happy and had nothing to complain about. In fact, I informed her, Tom's weaknesses were not nearly so bad as I'd made them out to be. That was the last time she asked me that question ...

If you let Him, God can perform the same miracle for you, making your heart the "grave" for the faults of your husband or wife. When we put something in the grave, we assume it is dead. If it resurfaces, that means we have buried it alive. If we do not put it to rest once and for all, it will continue to grow and strengthen.

Godly forgiveness can work in any heart that is willing to be set free from the burden of hurt, anger, animosity, and bitterness. These feelings

Finding Forgiveness

are deadly not only to a marriage, but more significantly to the individual that carries them.

I received a phone call one day from a woman that I could immediately tell was in a crisis. She told me through her tears that she had just learned that her husband had been unfaithful to her. She had questioned some of his behaviors in the past, but he had denied her concerns. He had lied and deceived her more than a few times, but now he had been caught. To make matters worse, the authorities were involved. Heartbroken, she expressed how hurt she was, as well as her anger and bitterness.

When she asked me what she should do, I paused a moment to pray and then asked, "Do you love him?"

"Yes, but I don't think that I can ever trust him again," she said. She went on to say some others who had learned of the situation were telling her she should leave him. He was no good, they said. He could never be trusted, and what's more, she needed to think of herself and the children.

She was in a state of confusion. While she loved him and wanted to save their marriage, she wanted to run away from the hurt and pain, the dishonesty and deception. After further discussion, I asked again if she loved her husband and wanted to save their marriage. She was willing but fearful. We talked about the forgiveness that God could put in her heart, and that her own love and forgiveness were insufficient to manage her circumstances. I told her God could make such a difference in how she handled the situation that her husband would see the change. I also helped her to see that one of the greatest ways to redeem her husband and help him find the complete victory in Christ would be through her love and forgiveness.

Together we read the verses, "Behold I am the LORD, the God of all flesh, is there anything too hard for Me?" *and* "With God all things are possible" (Jeremiah 32:27; Mark 10:27). As we talked further I could see she was becoming hopeful, eventually admitting she really didn't want to divorce her husband. With a willing spirit, she recognized that saving their marriage had as much to do with her as with him. Before closing the conversation, we prayed together, asking God to perform miracles, first in her own heart so she could forgive her husband and love and trust him again, and second for the transformed heart her husband so desperately needed.

For Better or For ~~Worse~~ Best

In the days that followed, this couple was in our prayers often. Not long after, the wife called again and said these simple but powerful words, "Alane, God's love is enough!" She went on to tell how she had taken our conversation to heart, asking God to give her the strength to do what she could not do herself—and He did!

As she demonstrated her love (which was really God's love) toward her husband, it broke his heart. He told her how he had tried to find victory, praying for years, but continuing to fail. Until he saw godly forgiveness demonstrated through his wife, he didn't believe God could help or forgive him. He gained hope through the love she displayed and, after confessing and repenting, found complete victory through the power of Jesus Christ. From that day forward they were a new couple, a restored couple, a happy couple. Praise God that this wife was willing to do the humanly impossible with God's help.

———•———

This couple's experience is not an isolated one. We personally know of many instances where God's love and power working through a willing spouse has saved a marriage, a home, and a family. What about you, dear reader? You may not be facing these kinds of circumstances in your marriage, but are you holding on to an unforgiving spirit, or a wounded heart? Whatever your circumstances, God's love is enough to see you through. All you have to do is be willing, and take hold of His love.

Perhaps, as you have read this chapter, the Holy Spirit has spoken to your heart. Maybe there is something you need to apologize for, or for which you should ask forgiveness. Perhaps the Holy Spirit has surprised you with the conviction that you have bitterness and an unforgiving spirit toward your spouse or some other person.

If this is your situation, Jesus tenderly entreats you, offering as a gift His own forgiving spirit in exchange for your bitterness and hurt. If you will only surrender your fears, your heartaches, the old lies you've come to believe, whatever it is, He has the power to provide a new heart and put His spirit within you!

Come to Him today to find forgiveness—whether it is the forgiveness you need to receive or the forgiveness you need to extend. He is willing and well able to supply every need!

Chapter Sixteen

Money Matters

When Alane and I married, we made a commitment to each other and God to return a 10% tithe and a 10% offering. At that time we both had good jobs and no children.

About a year after our marriage, we relied on both of our incomes to qualify for a mortgage and purchase a home. Our financial picture changed quickly about one week later when we found out Alane was pregnant. This was good news for us, but bad news for our bank account. We had made another foundational commitment when we married—that when we had children, Alane would leave her job to be a mother and homemaker. Now that we had a mortgage plus a baby on the way, there was potential for a real financial strain on our marriage.

The test came in two separate areas. First of all, would we be true to our commitment to God on tithes and offerings? Though cutting back on tithe was not an option for us, we could trim our offerings. We determined to stand by that 10% offering and see what God would do. What a joy and blessing over the last thirty years to see the fulfillment of God's word to "prove Me now herewith."

The second test was choosing between income and motherhood. Once again, we chose to stay true to our commitment, and once more we saw the hand of God proving true to His promise that "and all these things shall be added unto you."

In the early eighties, we took care of an elderly gentleman in our home whose philosophy on tithe was quite different than ours. Though he paid tithe on his "increase," his definition of increase was what he had left after he paid his taxes, bills, car payment, grocery bill, etc. We have watched other couples make this experiment as well, and the

For Better or For ~~Worse~~ Best

result always seems to be the same—there isn't much left for God, and they are always short on money.

In such situations, or whenever finances are tight, the topic can be pretty touchy. Many couples tend to "react" whenever the subject of money comes up. The wife may feel resentment because her husband spends money impulsively, leaving her without cash to buy needed household items. Some husbands feel their wife is an out-of-control shopper who doesn't consult them on spending. Other couples are plunged into tension and despair because, while one spouse is a saver, the other can't hold on to one extra dollar.

Because the need for money, the power that is often ascribed to it, and the love of it, attaches very closely to our SELF, disagreements about financial priorities are one of the main causes of marital discord. After couples get married, they find out how connected money and self really are—especially when there is a strong difference of opinion about how funds should be managed.

From a worldly perspective, money truly is power. God's Word addresses the attitudes that result from our selfish desires for more money and the power that comes with it in 1 Timothy 6:10: "The love of money is the root of all evil." This love of money, which can never be satisfied, is destructive to the "us first" attitude which is so important to a vibrant and loving marriage.

The good news is that our finances do matter to God—enough so that He has provided principles for the happy and effective management of both our money and hearts. In Matthew 6:33, Jesus advises us to "seek ye first the kingdom of God and His righteousness and all these things shall be added unto you." When we surrender our wills to God, seeking His ways, He will oversee our financial matters.

The first divinely provided money management principle is to:

Principle #1: Put God first financially

Malachi 3:10 says, "Bring ye all the tithes into the storehouse … and prove Me now herewith, saith the LORD of hosts, if I will not open you the windows of heaven, and pour you out a blessing, that there shall not be room enough to receive it." Here is both a command and a promise from God; a test of our willingness to actually put God's

Money Matters

directions and His cause first in our financial priorities. If we give back to God a "tithe" (10%) of what He has given us, we will discover what He means when He says He will open the windows of heaven and pour upon us His promised blessing.

This foundational principle is just as sure as God's word, yet how few professing Christians have enough trust and faith in Him to return an honest tithe. Our tithe should be the very first commitment we make after we are paid.

If you find yourself struggling to make ends meet, determine if you are truly putting God first. Are you surrendered to His will and dependent upon His power? Are you faithful in returning your tithes and offerings? His promises cannot, will not, fail!

There is another great financial pitfall that affects marriages today. It is an external pressure that stresses even the best of marriages and creates a bondage that is often either misunderstood or considered normal. This overbearing, relentless tyrant is called DEBT! Yes, debt, with its high interest rates and consuming background pressure, drives its victims to over-commitment and, often, emotional despair. This leads us to our next principle.

Principle #2: "Owe no man any thing" (Romans 13:8)

God gave us this principle because He knew how deadly debt is. In the words of the wise man, "The rich ruleth over the poor, and the borrower is servant to the lender" (Proverbs 22:7).

There is a cause-and-effect relationship between debt and servitude that we can easily understand. The borrower is subject to the demands and conditions of the lender. This is the basic reason to avoid debt. In the words of Benjamin Franklin, "When you run into debt, you give another person power over your liberty." Though Franklin's words sound very serious, they are true. For example, if you purchase a home and later default on the mortgage, the lender can sell the home to pay off the debt. If the home sells for more than you owe, you will be free of the debt. If it sells for less, however, you would still be liable for the difference.

"Frivolous debt," which we define as being incurred when there is not a compelling need for the debt (such as for furniture, recreational vehicles, vacations, etc.), can be even more dangerous. If you buy a new car and run into financial trouble three years later, the seller can repossess the car, sell it at a depreciated price, and still require you to pay off the remaining loan.

While the absence of debt is truly ideal, it wouldn't be possible for many couples to purchase a home without incurring some debt. The key is to evaluate your financial picture carefully. Then, after weighing the available options and opportunities, make the best decision for you.

If you do take out a mortgage, bend all your efforts to pay it off as quickly as possible. A couple with a $50,000, 30-year mortgage who pays extra on the principle each month can easily pay it off 10-20 years early, depending on the amount of extra they are able to pay. And what a difference it makes to be debt-free instead of still in financial bondage!

Couples who learn to manage their finances remove the number-one cause of marital conflict. This is a win/win situation—they will have more financial resources and experience greater marital harmony at the same time. In our own experience, we have found that having a budget (which is just another word for a financial "plan") is one of the best ways to ensure that we use money wisely. Though most people hate the idea of a budget, the likely alternative (serious financial trouble and the stress that goes with it) is also not very inviting.

Believe it or not, it is possible to have extra cash in your bank account at the end of each month. By following the steps already outlined in this chapter (avoiding debt and putting God first), then taking the simple steps below, you can be well on your way to financial freedom.

- *Step #1: Begin by listing your monthly income and expenses.*
- *Step #2: Prepare a budget, allocating amounts for each expense. Remember to budget amounts for bills that do not fall within the monthly cycle, such as property taxes, homeowner insurance, etc.*
- *Step #3: Stick to the budget you have set—avoid making exceptions.*

Money Matters

We encourage every married couple to make a budget and learn the discipline of living within that budget for at least one year. The blessing you will experience in stabilizing your finances as well as diminishing or eradicating conflict over money issues are well worth the effort involved. After just twelve months on a budget, we think you will experience such positive benefits that you will likely continue thereafter. In our experience, we have redeemed hundreds of dollars that would have vanished without a budget. We have also helped many couples develop a budget that meets their specific needs, and watched them as they obtained freedom and joy, as well! You may also benefit by implementing some of the cost-cutting measures below.

- **Insurance:** Shop around, compare policies, and ask for any hidden discounts, e.g., safe driver or senior, and good student discounts. Consider a higher deductible on both homeowner and vehicle insurance. Shop and save—every dollar saved is one less that needs to be earned. Most people can save **$200–$300/year** by shopping for competitive insurance rates.

- **Electricity:** Turn off any lights that are not in use and unplug power cords that still draw when an electronic device is not in use. Turn down the heat when you leave and at night while sleeping. These suggestions may seem like little things, but pennies add up to dollars day after day, week after week, and month after month. The average family can save $25.00 or more per month just by being attentive to energy-saving opportunities.

- ***Phone:*** *Re-evaluate your communication costs, including land lines, cell phone plans, Internet service and various related options. How many of these options do you really need or use? With careful evaluation, planning, and adjustment, the average family can save $20.00 or more each month on communication charges.*

For Better or For ~~Worse~~ Best

- **Water:** "Little" things such as how much water goes down the drain when you brush your teeth, whether you take a 5- or a 20-minute shower, or how many times you run the dishwasher all add up. Over a month's time, water consumption can really add up. Doing dishes by hand is another great money-saving option.

- **Garbage Pick-up:** If you are willing to sort your trash or recycle, you may be able to get by with biweekly or even monthly garbage service. We know a couple who take their plastic, aluminum, and paper to a recycling center, earning an average of $75-$100/year. Ask questions, find out your options, and see how creative you can be in reducing refuse removal expense.

- **Fuel:** Do we really have to drive as much as we do? Do we need to run to the store to get tortillas just because we have a hankering for tacos for dinner? For most families, nearly one-third of the gas budget is used for nonessentials or unnecessary driving. Through better planning, we can save time, money, and vehicle wear-and-tear by reducing the number of trips. The average family can save $50/month or more in gas expenses.

- **Home maintenance:** Most families can save a significant amount of money by doing their own housecleaning, painting, gutter cleaning, repairs, window washing, lawn mowing, and other household chores themselves rather than hiring them out. Making lawn care a family project is a good way to spend time together. What's more, many families could save $25 per week on lawn service alone.

- **Food:** Many families spend more than they need to on food by eating out often, buying prepackaged food, or going to the store when hungry (which encourages spending more than is needed). The average four-person family spends $100 per month extra on food due to impulse buying. Another $100 per month could be saved by taking advantage of sales, buying in bulk, using

Money Matters

coupons, and buying store brands. Hundreds could be saved by eating out once a quarter or twice a year, instead of daily or several times per week.

- **Pets:** Most people have no idea how much they spend on their pets each month. Food and vet bills add up quickly. If you don't have sufficient funds to feed your family or keep up with your bills you might consider foregoing pets until you can afford them.

- **Gifts:** While we may enjoy giving gifts, we need to carefully consider how much money we spend each year in this category. How can we continue to give without going over budget? Consider these ideas. For a Christmas get-together, draw names rather than buying each person a gift. Set a cap or a range that everyone agrees to. Consider practical, homemade gifts from your kitchen, garden, or workshop. Instead of buying $4 greeting cards, make your own or send an e-card instead.

- **Vacation:** Planning ahead is the key to remaining level-headed, avoiding impulse spending, and staying within a budget while on vacation. Begin with determining where you can afford to go, keeping in mind that creating fun memories does not have to cost a lot. Avoid the stress of facing credit card bills at the end of your trip by setting aside a little money each month to cover vacation expenses. Watch for travel deals that can save money as well, comparing online discount prices with travel agency rates. Do not assume that one source is always less expensive than the others.

By following the simple money-saving tips above, your family can save hundreds or even thousands of dollars per year. This "found" money can then be applied to credit card debt, mortgage principle, savings, your child's education, retirement, or helping others in need. Even if your income has not changed, with careful budgeting you can significantly reduce your debt. In addition, you will eliminate the stress of uncontrolled debt and the friction that results from this unnecessary

For Better or For ~~Worse~~ Best

pressure on your marriage. We've included a sample budget that can be modified for your family.

If you are weary of carrying the burden of your money matters, we invite you to apply God's principles to your financial scenario. If you are willing to surrender your will to the all-seeing eye and strength of God, you will experience a wonderful financial difference—through His power. God's ways are perfect. He will bring peace to our troubled hearts, and, when we put Him first this area of our life, He will make a success of our "money matters."

Money Matters

Managing Money Sample Budget Sheet

Sample Income			Your income
	$4,500.00		
Tithe 10%	$450.00		
Rental/Home Loan	$950.00		
Home Insurance	$30.00	($360/yr)	
Credit card/other debt	$350.00		
RX/health insurance	$200.00		
Property Tax	$170.00	($2000/yr)	
Utilities (electric, water, garbage pickup, etc)	$325.00		
Cell phone	$99.00		
Land line phone/cable/internet	$114.00		
Vehicle payment	$250.00		
Auto insurance	$50.00	($600/yr)	
Licensing fees	$17.00	($200/yr)	
Auto maintenance	$25.00		
Fuel	$200.00		
Groceries	$725.00		
Household exp (cleaning, paper products, etc)	$35.00		
Home décor	$25.00		
Clothing	$75.00		
Gifts/cards	$45.00		
Yard/garden/lawn maintenance	$50.00		
Pets	$30.00		
Entertainment	$25.00		
Vacation	$150.00		
Dining	$50.00		
School supplies	$10.00		
Professional Licensing			
Educational savings			
Savings	**$50.00**		
	$0.00		

Restoration International
www.restoration-international.org

Chapter Seventeen

Managing Emotions

*E*arly in our marriage, managing my emotions was a particular challenge for me. If Tom didn't respond agreeably to my mood, I assumed he didn't really care about me. My overactive imagination also frequently inspired me to believe that others were more important to him than I was. I learned the hard way that choosing to dwell on worrisome and anxious thoughts can often bring them to pass. Such self-fulfilling prophecies are described in Ministry of Healing, pg. 360. "Often it is our own attitude, the atmosphere that surrounds ourselves, which determines what will be revealed to us in another."

When I read that simple, straightforward principle, it spoke to my heart. I realized it was likely that my own attitude and emotions had "set the table" for Tom's response. When I felt insecure or sorry for myself, the atmosphere I conveyed prepared the way for him to respond in the way I feared.

Over the years I have learned to stop making excuses for why I might be unhappy, upset, angry, discouraged, depressed, or frustrated. Now I understand that there is no excuse for sin—no excuse for allowing our circumstances to control our feelings. It is simply a **choice** we make. No matter how challenging the circumstances may be, our response still boils down to our choice. Though God has provided all power under heaven to deliver us from temptation, it remains our choice whether to accept it or not.

The issue of thought control is a problem in many marriages, especially for women. One woman I know, who let her imagination run wild, concluded that her husband didn't love or care for her. She also decided that she—and her children—would be better off without him. I advised her to ask God for the victory over those thoughts and emotions, before they literally became her reality, destroying both her and her marriage.

For Better or For ~~Worse~~ Best

She refused, and continued to let her thoughts run wild, until she was convinced she would be better off alone.

Not long afterward, her husband, who was frustrated and hurt that she wouldn't believe him when he expressed his love for her, left and eventually divorced her.

"I thought I would be better off, but I'm not," she told me soon after the divorce. "I have lost my marriage and home, and now I am worse off than I was before." She regretted not dealing with her thoughts and emotions, but it was too late.

Like many others, this woman blamed her husband—and circumstances—rather than coming face to face with the deception of the natural heart, which Jeremiah 17:9 tells us is "deceitful above all things, and desperately wicked." The key is to take hold of God's promised power, asking Him to do in us what it is impossible for us to do without Him. This is the only way to find true peace and happiness. What is truly amazing is that, when we surrender to God, we will find our love and respect for our spouse growing even if they are not changing!

Now is the time to surrender those recorded lies that circulate through our minds and only bring discouragement, frustration, and despair. In God's Word we are advised to cast down "imaginations, and every high thing that exalteth itself against the knowledge of God, and bringing into captivity every thought to the obedience of Christ" (2 Corinthians 10:5). God's Word is very clear about how we are to treat and think of each other in our marriages. When we let our thoughts run unchecked and our emotions to spin out of control, we dishonor God and our marriage.

It is a known psychological principle that emotions start first with thoughts, which in turn lead to feelings. In the words of Solomon, "As he thinketh in his heart so is he" (Proverbs 23:7).

Once, I decided to test the principle that "thoughts lead to emotions." I began thinking about someone who didn't like me. In fact, they called me names and even spread false reports about me. Amazingly, I quickly began to recognize physical changes in myself in response to my thoughts. My heart was beating faster, respiration was shorter and

Managing Emotions

faster, I had feelings of uneasiness and anxiety, and my blood pressure increased. The more I thought about the details, the worse I felt. I ended the experiment quickly, by calling out to God to deliver me from those thoughts—which He did!

This experiment confirmed that the connection between thoughts and emotions was not only true, but unavoidable. It also helped me to realize how badly I need to give my burdens and pain to Christ, so that my thoughts wouldn't cause me to respond the way I did. Jesus wants to heal us of our wrong thought processes and the emotions that accompany them. He also wants to heal us of the hurts, fears, animosity, and bitterness that result from what others have done to us. Though we can't change others or how they choose to treat us, by the grace of God we can choose to control how our thoughts and our emotions respond.

The level of control that we can have over our own spirits, through a vital connection to Christ, is nothing short of amazing. With His help, we can choose how we will respond to harsh or cutting words. We can govern the thoughts that spontaneously come to us, deciding if the emotion to which we are tempted to succumb is acceptable. When we handle our thoughts and emotions in this way, people or circumstances cannot make us angry, hurt our feelings, or make us fearful and anxious. By choosing how we will respond ahead of time, we can react according to God's grace when temptation does come. The experience described by Isaiah can be ours: "Thou wilt keep him in perfect peace, whose mind is stayed on Thee: because he trusteth in Thee" (Isaiah 26:3).

───────●───────

I had the opportunity to put my emotion-management skills to the test in 1995, when the doctors diagnosed me with ovarian cancer. This news, which would have been upsetting for anyone, was particularly challenging at that stage of my life. I was thirty-eight years old at the time, and our children were young. Among other things, I wanted to be there for them!

Though I had learned early in our marriage to follow the prescription of Philippians 4:8 with regard to my thoughts, this new trial called for a deeper understanding of that principle.

For Better or For ~~Worse~~ Best

Whenever I started to think of what my future might hold, my thoughts would spin out of control and emotions would overtake me. In that hour of need, I realized just how much I needed to trust in God to give me the grace to go through whatever was best for me and my family. As I surrendered myself and the unknown future more fully to God, He gave me peace.

I remember the day Alane had her surgery. A medical expert from UCLA Medical Center, whose specialty was removing cancers without allowing them to spread, had been brought in.

As the hours ticked by, I sat in the surgical waiting room. During that time, my mind wandered to such thoughts as, "Alane may only have six months to live. What about the children?" Then I would hear God calling to me to trust Him, together with the reassurance that He would never leave or forsake me.

Finally, the time came when the waiting room receptionist called me to meet the surgeons. That was an intense moment of trusting my dear wife and my emotions to my Heavenly Father. He kept my heart and gave me peace to face the reality of the unknown. Alane didn't have cancer! I rejoiced at the wonderful news and for God's power to keep my emotions trusting in Him.

After my surgery, we were told that the tumor was not malignant. I did have an extreme case of endometriosis, however, and all of my female organs had been removed. Within just a few days, my hormone levels plummeted as my body went into crisis menopause. As a result, my emotions were thrown into chaos.

I recognized this challenge, and, by the grace of God (and with much prayer and many difficult choices), I found victory over the emotions that struggled for the mastery. Determining not to use my hormonal imbalance and unstable emotions as an excuse for my words, actions, or reactions, I chose to allow God to give me the strength for each new circumstance and day. Even when my heart didn't feel like it, I learned to develop a calm sense of peace.

Managing Emotions

The next time you are in a situation that involves conflict, or tempts you to begin thinking negative thoughts, choose to surrender those thoughts and your entire self to Christ. Ask Him to help you to see things as He sees them and then turn your thoughts to "whatsoever things are true, whatsoever things are honest, whatsoever things are just, whatsoever things are pure, whatsoever things are lovely, whatsoever things are of a good report … think on these things" (Philippians 4:8).

Though emotions were given to us by God as a blessing, they are a means of expression that should be governed appropriately and not allowed to control us. It is essential that we bring our thoughts and emotions under the control of Christ, but this can only happen when we submit our will to Him.

If you are not surrendered to Christ, now is the time, today is the day of salvation. Jesus not only has the solution to your emotional needs, He has the answer to every aspect of your life—including making your marriage the best.

Chapter Eighteen

Resolving Conflict

On one occasion, a family came to our home to discuss the problems they were having with their teenagers. It was evident that these young people had strong negative attitudes and an uncooperative spirit. As the parents shared their challenges and concerns, Tom and I became aware of the discord between the husband and wife. Accordingly, we asked to speak with the parents alone.

During that conversation, the husband was very cold and disconnected from his wife. He also spoke to her sharply.

"Do you love your wife?" I asked him.

"No, I never did," he replied with a coldness that shocked me. "I've just been sticking it out for 20 years, and I can't take it anymore." He went on to say he was planning to leave her, justifying his plans by saying that it would be better for them and for the children. All this was shared in front of his wife, who had tears rolling down her cheeks. Untouched by her breaking heart, he seemed to steel himself in his decision.

"Why can't you love her?" I asked, looking directly at him.

"I've tried, but it doesn't work," was his unfeeling response.

Silently praying for wisdom, I responded, "I know you can't love her. You have proven that already. But God can put His love in your heart for her. God's love is divine. It can love even the most unlovely and unlovable. Human love alone is not enough, but divine love coupled with human love is more than enough."

The man listened as his wife was grasping for hope.

Tom then told them that the key to happiness in our marriage had been Luke 9:24: "For whosoever will save his life shall lose it: but whosoever will lose his life for My sake, shall save it." He went on to talk about the "me" focus—casting blame, justifying our words and actions,

For Better or For ~~Worse~~ Best

self-serving, always being right—and how it never brings real peace. Tom also encouraged this husband to surrender himself to God and learn to live in the "us" focus.

We could see him wrestling with making a decision. The battle in his heart was very visible in his countenance. Satan—together with this man's natural, selfish heart—was pushing him to give up on his marriage. But God, through His Holy Spirit—that still small voice that speaks to our conscience—was drawing him to remain and recommit to love his wife.

Later he told us—and these are his own words—"You probably do not know how close I was to the edge of the deep canyon, ready to jump down into the darkness. You probably remember how rebellious I was at your home, but you held your peace and remained calm and firm … when Alane asked me, with tears in her eyes, why I couldn't love my wife—her words nearly pierced my heart. At your family campmeeting I was impressed with the messages, but there was still a resistance in my heart that I could not explain. But that resistance was taken away from me slowly—message after message—until it was completely removed. When Tom approached me one week later and asked if I was committed I said 'Yes!' He shared that he had been praying that I would become committed. I then told Tom, 'This is my commitment: I will do everything, go anywhere, and leave nothing undone to see my wife and each of my children in heaven.'"

It has been more than six years since that commitment was made, and it is nothing less than a modern-day miracle to see the change in this man's heart, the change in his marriage, his family, his life and his influence on others. By the power of a living God and his own personal choice, that man's heart was changed. His marriage and family were saved, and today they are ministering to others about the saving power of the Gospel of Christ.

When this family first came to visit us, their son was nearly eighteen years old. "I'll be 'out of here' (his home) as soon as I'm 18 years old," he boldly told us. But after witnessing the miraculous change in his father, the son's heart was also changed. Instead of leaving home in rebellion, he became a respectful, obedient son.

Resolving Conflict

This man's wife—who had held on by a thin thread of hope—now has a husband who truly loves her. A man's soul saved, a marriage saved, a family saved, all through the redeeming power of a personal Savior—what could be more rewarding and thrilling!

This is a dramatic story, yet not really hard to believe if we understand the key or solution to the problem. It is no less than a surrender of self to Jesus and an acceptance of Him to be master of our heart and will. If we are willing to surrender, He can teach us how to love, forgive, and be made whole. If we choose to hold on to our selfish nature, justifying our words and actions and excusing our wrongs, we will be as miserable as this man once was. Self is a very difficult and demanding taskmaster!

In working with this family and their teenagers, Tom and I were simply following a Bible principle for conflict resolution that was offered by God Himself. Found in the first chapter of Isaiah, it reads, "Come now, and let us reason together, saith the L<small>ORD</small>*" (Verse 18).*

Though very short, this simple phrase conveys three very important concepts.

First, "come" is an invitation—an appeal. It conveys there must be a willingness on the part of both parties to come—a desire to seek resolution. Next, the words "let us reason" indicate openness and frankness. This involves thinking things through logically, discussing them, and listening without defending, raising our voice, or putting the other person down. Last, "together" speaks of a desire for harmony, unity, and the blending of two hearts—"the two shall become one." This is what marriage is all about and following this principle results in conflict resolution in Christ.

Because of human nature, all married couples have experienced conflict to some degree. The remedy for conflict as described above may seem simple, but it really does work. All too often it is the small things that go unresolved—those things that are placed in the back corner of our hearts, but continue to grow quietly, perhaps even unperceived at first. Given enough time, however, they will break out with force in words or actions that are not in proportion to the original problem, leaving deep hurts and even greater misunderstanding.

For Better or For ~~Worse~~ Best

*We have learned, by experience, that whether disagreements are large or small, it is **how we choose to respond to that conflict** that will make the difference between success and failure in our marriage. By coming together, reasoning together, listening to each other, and doing it all in a spirit of harmony, we have come to a point where disagreements and conflict are rare in our relationship. Through God's grace, we expect to continue that pattern of peace and harmony in our home, and the good news is that by applying the principles in God's Word, you can have this experience too.*

When counseling is needed

Throughout this book we have shared practical principles that work. They have worked (and continue to work) in our marriage and many other marriages with which we are personally acquainted. Though there is transforming power in Jesus, there are times, for a multitude of reasons, that one or both spouses feel inadequate, discouraged, overwhelmed, helpless, or in some other way unprepared to resolve the problems in their marriage. In such cases, there is a place for restorative and godly Bible-based counseling. Should you find yourself in a situation where you believe you need counseling to restore your marriage, please consider these key points to ensure success:

1) **Desire the restoration of your marriage**

This means your only intention is to seek a solution, not to obtain sympathy. This also means that you are going in with an open mind, willing to see "my" problem, not just your spouse's problems.

2) **Seek an unbiased and confidential counselor**

In most cases, friends and family members are not an unbiased source. To avoid your situation being in the next week's "gossip material," choose a counselor who will keep your issues strictly confidential. One couple we counseled had confided in their pastor one week, only to find out the next week that several other church members were privy to their issues. Understandably, they were quite hesitant to seek

Resolving Conflict

counseling again! Proceed carefully and prayerfully when choosing a counselor.

3) Seek counseling based on biblical principles

If you do decide to seek a counselor, make sure you prayerfully choose one whose counsel is solidly based on biblical principles. This is very important, since today's popular or modern psychology is so destructive. We counseled with one couple where the wife had been repeatedly sexually abused throughout much of her childhood and teenage years. The professional counsel she received recommended she write out the details of her abuse as a means for processing and discarding the memories. Needless to say, this recommendation did not work. This is not to say that we should not identify the cause of our issues. However, pushing someone to concentrate on reliving and journaling the details of their negative experiences complicates the recovery process. Writing things down merely makes them more permanent in our memory.

In Philippians 3:13, 14 we are admonished, "Forgetting those things which are behind, and reaching forth unto those things which are before, I press toward the mark for the prize of the high calling of God in Christ Jesus."

Once this woman identified her mistrust of men (which unfortunately included her innocent husband) as the basis of her problems, she began the process of building trust and believing the truth about who she was in Christ. She also began to recognize the old lies as temptations that should be given to Christ and no longer listened to or believed. Today she has a beautiful marriage and family; a powerful testimony to the cleansing and healing power of Jesus Christ.

In summary: If you and/or your spouse choose to seek counseling, we recommend that you approach it with a sincere desire for the restoration of your marriage, and only through confidential counseling that is based on sound biblical principles.

For Better or For ~~Worse~~ Best

In order to resolve conflict we need to be surrendered to Christ, choose to let go of the "me" focus, open our hearts to each other, and reason together in lowliness of mind … esteeming others better than ourselves" (Philippians 2:3).

We also need to choose to allow Christ to give us the grace to handle our emotions instead of being driven by our natural negative emotional responses. What we think in our hearts constitutes who we actually are. This is why it is essential we bring every thought to the obedience and control of Christ.

It is exciting to realize with Christ all things **are** possible and that we can move from marital conflict to marital bliss and fulfillment! We can have the marriages that Christ desires for each of us—not just a better marriage, the best—a marriage heart-to-heart.

Chapter Nineteen

Keeping Love Alive

When we are in the excitement of courtship, keeping love alive is the least of our worries. Love simply grows, and those attentions that keep it alive seem to spring forth spontaneously. But somehow after the honeymoon is over, life with all its press and cares begins to obstruct those expressions of love. At first, for us, the symptoms weren't obvious. We weren't talking as much as we did before. Or we were busy with those things that really had to be done, though yesterday's disagreement did cause us to be a little withdrawn today. In addition, things that we once expressed appreciation for were now easy to take for granted. When we united in marriage, we didn't understand how "me"-focused and selfish we were.

"I would never treat my wife that way," was a comment I remember well, made by one of my closest friends. Alane and I were having a difficult time during our first year of marriage, and my friend had noticed some things he didn't like.

He was engaged at the time, and I knew he was sincere. But though I had also been sincere, I had never anticipated some of the struggles we were experiencing. Unfortunately, it wasn't very long into my friend's marriage that they were facing previously unknown areas of their hearts and struggling as well.

The love between a husband and wife does not automatically stay alive and healthy. It is like a plant that needs nourishment, tender care, and protection. First it takes knowledge of how to nourish and care for it. Then it takes a conscious commitment and purposeful follow-through to faithfully carry out those intentions. In our own experience, we have found six simple, yet powerful and practical suggestions that truly do keep love alive and growing:

For Better or For ~~Worse~~ Best

1. Little attentions often

Luke 16:10 says, "He that is faithful in that which is least is faithful also in much." When we were dating, we undoubtedly did many special things to express our love and capture the heart of our spouse. Not letting those little attentions fade away is one of the simplest, yet most effective ways we can keep love alive and growing. Don't be ruled by your feelings: they follow actions and are subject to change. By choosing to take action even when you don't feel like it, you will experience the blessings God has in store for you. The sum of life's happiness is made up of the little things!

There are many places where thoughtful, loving, and affectionate notes can be tucked. Lunch bags, laptop cases, briefcases, in a book or Bible, under the pillow, or on the bathroom mirror are just a few of the handy places we've found.

When your spouse leaves for work you can walk them to the door, and when they come home, meet them there with a kiss. Wave at the window, have prayer together, hang up their coat, or sweep out the garage. Helping with the children, watering the plants, and making the bed are all other ways to show your spouse that you care.

You can also show love by taking care of yourself. When you wear cologne or keep yourself attractive (e.g. clean, neat, and orderly in both clothes and body), that sends a message to your spouse!

Alane and I were enjoying a few hours together at the lake one afternoon. While she relaxed in the sun, I searched for some heart-shaped rocks. I thought these small tokens would be a simple way to express my love and let her know I was thinking about her. When I proudly presented the collection with my expressions of love, her response told me this "little attention" hit the mark for keeping love alive.

---

2. Regular, daily communication

Hebrews 13:16: "To communicate forget not: for with such sacrifices God is well pleased." Consistent communication is one of the best

Keeping Love Alive

ways to keep love alive. Regular, daily communication is more than just saying, "Good morning," or "Did you get the bills paid?" It is real heart-level communication that conveys to your spouse that you love them, appreciate them, and are interested in them. This means that we need to have a set time every day for communication.

We had to literally put this commitment in our daily schedule in order to make it happen. Saying we wanted or needed time to talk wasn't enough. Setting a time each day, and then keeping our commitment, accelerated our relationship towards being truly heart-to-heart.

During this special time of uninterrupted communication we share our joys, our challenges, our disappointments, and our hearts. We talk about the real issues and needs of life. We resolve misunderstandings, problem solve, and plan for the future of our family. Through this time together we develop habits of communication and establish our way of operating as husband and wife. This gives our daily life stability and meaning. As a result, we have come to understand and know each other on a much deeper level; often to the extent we know what the other is thinking and can anticipate each others needs before they are even expressed.

The time period you choose doesn't matter, although we don't recommend bedtime since it's too easy to fall asleep. The time just needs to be one that works for you and your spouse. It may be following the evening meal, right after you get home from work, during your daily walk time, or sometime around evening worship. The key is to set a time and stick with it.

If you have trouble finding things to talk about, consider expressing appreciation for any of the following, or more ...

- *Nice, healthy meals*
- *A clean vehicle*
- *A neat, orderly home*
- *Interest in the children*
- *Pleasant home atmosphere*
- *Personal appearance*
- *Helpfulness*

For Better or For ~~Worse~~ Best

- *Cheerfulness*
- *Timeliness*
- *Sensitivity to the needs of others*

You may show how important your spouse is to you by adding just one or two of these types of comments into your conversations each day and notice the difference it makes in your own heart as well as in your relationship.

- *"You are the most wonderful man in the world to me."*
- *"You are the joy of my life."*
- *"You are the most important person to me."*
- *"I love spending time with you."*
- *"I've been thinking about you a lot today."*
- *"I appreciate your input (or perspective)."*
- *"You are the one for me."*
- *"We were made for each other."*

---

3. Time together for each other

As we found out, there is a difference between BEING together and being TOGETHER. The state of being "together in the same room" is not the same as "being together" in the same room. If one of you is reading the newspaper and the other is on the computer in the same room, you are together, but you're not being together in a way that will make love grow.

While there is a place for "separate togetherness," the struggle in most marriages today involves whether the couple has **any** time together **at all**. Couples used to say "well, we do sleep together," but now many times we don't even hear that. Instead we hear, "My husband sits at the computer well into the night after I go to bed."

In the world in which we live, a multitude of pressures and distractions do vie for our time and attention. However, if we are going to keep love alive by doing things together, we need to make a commitment and ask God to help us accomplish our goal. Personally, I have a commitment to God and to my family that I won't add even one new responsibility without first consulting Him and Alane as to where the time would come from. I was the kind of person that would say "yes" to just about anyone or anything, so I have to guard against this.

Once, when a church committee member called and asked me to take another church office, I declined, explaining that my first commitment was to God and my family. The church committee was shocked that I actually said no to their request, but they were very impressed with my reasons why. The time I gained as a result of making this simple decision was put into developing my relationship and trust in God and building my marriage and family.

Being careful to avoid over-commitment has brought greater balance into my life and, as a result, I have found it possible to accomplish more than before, both inside and outside the home. Alane now knows that she is the first priority in my life, and there is no one on earth that I would rather spend my time with.

As I reflect on how we spend time together and do things for each other as husband and wife, I understand in a deeper way the meaning of the words of Christ, "The two shall become one."

Perhaps your situation is different than ours. You may not work side-by-side in ministry or spend much of your days together. Our life wasn't that way in earlier years either. Yet we have found that, no matter what situation you find yourselves in, you can make more time for each other. You can turn over a "new leaf" now, by taking time to evaluate your commitments. If you don't set aside time for your marriage and family, you can be sure that other people's needs and demands will sweep you away. You can guard against this, by making a plan before you close the day. Pray for God to guide in your exciting new commitment to keep love alive!

---

4. Keep love alive by anticipation

While surprises and spontaneity are fun, anticipation is also good for our relationship. I remember clearly the weeks and days before we were married; anticipating our wedding day, the honeymoon, and our new life together. If we plan ahead for a weekend getaway, a dinner out, a vacation or a retreat, we build special memories that will be attached to these special events, making them meaningful and memorable. This planning also helps us to focus on positive thoughts instead of the negative ones that all too easily find root in our hearts.

5. Praying together

Praying together is an integral part of the marriage relationship. When we are willing to open up our hearts before God and each other, to humble ourselves and be transparent, it creates a spiritual intimacy that strengthens our love. The end result is a deeper understanding and compassion for one another.

This prayer time should not be generic, ritualistic, or rote prayers. Rather, they are an expression of appreciation for specific things, an open request for guidance, and an honest confession of our wrongs and failures combined with a request for forgiveness and help. As a result of this prayer time that Tom and I spend together, we have understood each other more deeply. In addition, a corresponding respect and appreciation has grown which not only keeps love alive, but increases its depth, as well.

If you're not used to sharing a prayer time with your spouse, you may feel a bit uncomfortable at first. Don't let this awkwardness deter you. Approach this time together as an opportunity to be real, honest, and forthright! Your spouse will appreciate your vulnerability and honesty and will know better how to pray for you, respond to, and understand you.

If you hear something during this time that you weren't previously aware of, don't get upset or hurt. Recognize the openness and vulnerability of your spouse as an opportunity to communicate about the subject. Show sympathy and interest, concern and compassion, rather than an accusing spirit, hurt or anger. How you respond in this critical moment will make the issue either easy or difficult to resolve. Responding in a more positive way doesn't mean you are justifying or excusing a wrong, but rather seeking to restore the wrongdoer. God Himself will help us learn to respond His way, and as a result our hearts will be bound together, just as they are bound to Him through prayer and communion.

Keeping Love Alive

6. Daily affection

Love can't survive long in a cold, sunless environment with no affection. We all need the warmth of a caring touch—yet how many couples forget to daily express affection to their spouse through a loving glance, thoughtful kiss, or warm embrace? While husbands are more likely to focus on impulsive intimacy, wives are especially desirous of gentle, meaningful affection. And those gentle affections, shared throughout the day, set the tone for much richer and more meaningful intimacy in the evening.

Before we get out of bed every morning, Alane and I start the day cuddling. We express our appreciation for each other, and thank our Heavenly Father for providing the one by our side. After we finish our personal devotional time, we come together again for a special time of reading and prayer together, followed by an affectionate hug.

When the blessing for the food has been asked, I like to give Alane a kiss of gratitude for the meal she has prepared, and the blessing she is to me as a "helpmeet."

As we go through the day, we share spontaneous thoughts of appreciation and touches of kindness and affection—a message that we care for each other. At the close of the day, we pray together again. Then we kiss, hug, and have our nighttime snuggle before going to sleep.

In 1 Corinthians 7:3, Paul advises couples that the husband should "render to his wife the affection due her, and likewise also the wife to her husband." Husbands who want the best marriage will express this affection daily, not on their own terms, but according to the needs of the wife—the "affection due her."

Researchers for a life insurance company once conducted a study that came up with some truly fascinating results. The researchers discovered that husbands who kiss their wives every morning:

- Live an average of 5 years longer
- Are involved in fewer automobile accidents

For Better or For ~~Worse~~ Best

- Take 50% less sick days
- Earn 20-30% more income

Other research has found that thoughtful kisses and hugs release endorphins which give the mind and body a sense of genuine well-being. While a kiss a day may keep the doctor away, it will, more importantly, keep love alive! Keeping our love alive means keeping our marriage alive. All the real life experiences and principles we have shared in this book have been and continue to be a big part of making our marriage vibrant with love.

As we come to the close of this book, our prayer and the desire of our hearts for you is that you won't just have a better marriage but the best—a marriage that is heart-to-heart.

For more information about building your marriage heart to heart to make it the BEST:

Order:
Marriage Heart-to-Heart DVD
26 programs

Visit us online:
www.restoration-international.org

Call toll free:
1-888-446-8844

Write:
Restoration International
PO Box 2150
Eureka, MT 59917-2150